CHEZ
Mwah

Judith Dowden

DEDICATION

I dedicate this book to my own Mr Rigsby,
without whose careful accounting, this Place
In The Sun would have remained nothing
more than a French Fancy

CONTENTS

THINGS TO DO, PLACES TO GO

All information accurate at the time of writing

ACKNOWLEDGMENTS

Thanks to Languedoc Living and
Charlotte Craig for not laughing.

Except when she was supposed to.

1: SKIVING OVER MELONS

We've all enjoyed an afternoon under the duvet with Peter Mayle and a turn at the wheel of driving over lemons.

But there's another tranche of books about a fantasy life Sur le Continent. They are the froth on the café crème of the genre. The lead characters are predominantly women, spurned, redundant and helpless, who buy houses on impulse, after a brief holiday during which they have an epiphany.

If they bought that little run down cottage/apartment it would change their lives/bodies/wardrobe.

The first thing they do when they move in, after a purchase as painless as buying a pack of apero snacks – more often than not the first property they ever looked at – is that they "throw open" the shutters. The idea of "flinging" open shutters to let in "beams of sunlight" which "penetrate the room" is a cliché so well hackneyed it brings on an outbreak of hives. In reality if I flung, threw, tossed or attempted any other projectile movement with my own weather worn volets, they'd would either snap right back and give me a black eye, pinch my chipolata fingers in their splintered grip or simply disintegrate into a thousand pieces.

Out of work actors and fading daytime TV stars seem to have a penchant for churning out this stuff. (I was at school with one of them. 55 my arse.) When their protagonists have finished hurling their shutters around in gay abandon, they "whip" off the dust covers, render the windows "sparkling" with the merest flick of a chamois, before popping down to their ever open and plentiful (yeah right) baker. They wander, basket over arm, round the "bustling" market (shut two hours ago, love). On returning to their "quirky" yet homely kitchen, they conjure up a simple, gourmet lunch and sip a glass of local wine in the flower-filled courtyard. (The weeding fairies must have visited in the night.) Breathing in the hibiscus (doesn't smell) they tip their "remarkably young for her age" faces to the sun and think about how lucky (smug) they are.

Well, call me bitter and twisted......oh......you actually ARE!.......but when I eventually arrive at my house (at the vagaries of the air traffic controllers), bleached the smell of cat poo from the front step, scrubbed the mold from the bedroom wall and crawled maniacally around every skirting board for paranoid-imagined evidence of droppings, I'm buggered if I'm going to be cooking anything.

With my crushed and bleeding stumps (OK so I did try the shutter thing) I curl back the lid of a tin of two year old cassoulet, open the last bottle of wince inducing wine remaining from last time – there was a reason we left it – and collapse in front of the telly. Even this looses its appeal after half an hour as the telly isn't actually on.

Due to very early onset dementia, the husband has forgotten how to connect it up.

The annoying thing is, I'm a sucker for all those books, in the ever optimistic hope that one might actually have a hint of realism or even, heaven forefend, a decent storyline. Yes, I fall for those covers with their jaunty line drawings of thin, glamorous women trotting past the cafe in chic heels and frilly dresses. Surely it's what I DO actually look like to people, when I'm galumphing around the village in my egg stained cardigan? Oh, that friendly cursive script delivering tortuous puns and innuendo.

"Je ne regrette Rihanna."

"Yes we Cannes!"

"Oui Oui in La Vie".

There are quotes of praise from other, more established writers, lending credibility.

"Fabulously enjoyable" …….compared to having your eyes poked out with a corkscrew.

"A light hearted romp" …….vacuous and facile.

"A genuine taste of France" ……..nothing like it.

To cover all bases and make as many royalties as possible they might throw in the odd murder, or even a recipe. NO! Is that how you make a French dressing? Egg Mayonnaise? REALLY? I would never have guessed. You've changed my life and let's get on to the estate agent.

So, you are hissing, if you're so bloody clever why don't you write one yourself? Well, you know what, that's exactly what I'm doing right now, so I bet you're sorry.

"Skiving over Melons.

A light hearted romp about a menopausal Francophile, whose holiday home in the Languedoc promises to change her life and enable her to follow her ambition of throwing open the shutters before avoiding all housework and mainly lying on the sofa eating Jaffa Cakes. The Jaffa Cakes are bought from the English shelf of her otherwise typically French corner shop, run by the twinkly eyed Monsieur who, kisses her on both cheeks even when she goes in with a long shopping list at one minute to twelve. Midday. Lunchtime.

To complete her dream, she'll watch endless daytime television – oops – apart from the hilarious stumbling block that her husband can't get the television to work. What a typically English character! Chuckle as you follow his bumbling attempts to join two wires together.

There is even crime and intrigue. What bastard ate the last Jaffa Cake?

There is a bonus recipe. Discover the secret of making that typically French dish, salade de tomate. Described in easy to follow steps, it will have your guests gasping with wonder at your general typical Frenchness."

It'll make me millions and then I'll buy a huge, better house with staff that can clean in preparation for my linen-clad arrivage. They can light crackling fires; leave a Daube bubbling on the old stove; make up enormous, squashy beds with crisp linen; scatter vases brimming with blooms from my manicured, fragrant garden. Everything would be polished, preened and perfect. Everything would work.

The trouble with that is though, what would I do?

More importantly, what would I have to moan about?

And what would Mr Rigsby do? What exactly would he be for? What would be on his list of jobs? Nothing, that's what, which means he'd just be hanging around all day and we can't have that.

Anyway, I do quite like being Snow White. It's actually really satisfying to wake up a house that's been cold and dormant all Winter, let in air, breathe life into it. I love the smell of a French cleaning product and the billow of a newly laundered sheet. As I throw open the shutters, beams of yellow sunshine light up the dust motes as they float through the air. I wipe the Winter grime from the windows and sweep away the …….oh blimey I'm at it now…….where are the Jaffa Cakes?

2: PAINTING ANTS

One rainy English afternoon, the husband had cried off work with a touch of man flu and whiled away an hour watching "A Place in the Sun" for the restorative effect of second hand vitamin D.

Of course, personally, I don't watch daytime television. Occasionally, when one is dusting the controls, the screen might pop itself on by accident. It seems churlish then to switch it off. After all, they've gone to all the trouble to make that cookery show, bought all the food and everything and, if there's one thing I hate it's waste. Or they might have gathered a shell besuited crowd together to make over a semi in Chingford. Well, if nobody watches them they might turn ugly.

One of my many, many bugbears in life is that those who go on "A Place in the Sun" are infinitely imbecilic. All they can ever think of to do on that terrace is "imagine myself with a glass of wine." Don't get me going on "We didn't bother learning French but we want to be part of a community". But, worst of all and the thing that gets me throwing Victoria Sponge at the telly – (best scenario in which to watch "A Place in the Sun" – prostrate on sofa, wedge of Victoria Sponge, mug of tea) the VERY worst thing is that Barry and Brenda from Solihull come over all estate agency.

Instead of saying, as they would in real life, "Bugger me, Brenda, this gaff's enormous!" they come out with "Well, Jasmine, it's a good size room, with a double aspect and lots of potential". Also the producers make them all hold hands. Before my application to appear on "A Place in the Sun" was unfathomable rejected – I mean, who wouldn't find me fascinating? – I had already made up my mind that I'd refuse to hold hands.

Anyhow, my husband's fancy was particularly taken with a nice couple, mincing around the Limousin in a linen trouser and snapping up a three story house for less than the price of a weekend on Eurostar.

(Special price £59 return my arse. Show me one person who's ever actually found that!)

Next thing, we were bombing around the country lanes of the French countryside, a couple of bemused kids in tow. Those were the days when they would follow you anywhere without question, little rucksacks packed, eyes wide with wonder and adoration, ready to believe anything you said. Nowadays I hear them scheming about how to get a pillow over our faces before we sell the house to support our indefinite existence in a twilight home.

We were shown farmhouses with barns, ginormous lofts, streams, fields and their own woods. But what would we do with a field? It would take Mr Rigsby our entire minibreak to mow it and we've only got a Hover. So we spurned them all and found a little cottage with a toiny garden. We bought a little bit more garden from a bloke called Gael – turned out he was the only "Gael in the Village". There was a long evening of negotiations over a litre of Pinet, at which one had to talk about everything else in the world – well, the new chef at the restaurant, the state of Gael's leeks and his new tractor – before plucking up courage to broach the subject of the garden. Then it was a quick un, deux, trois - settle on a price, a bit on the side for Gael and we left as land owners.

On one side lived Charles, who was the ex-mayor. This wasn't such a big deal as we found out that everyone had been the mayor. He used to pop up from behind his hedge in his big old straw hat whenever we came and went and leave frilly balls of lettuce on the kitchen doorstep. Marie and her son Christophe lived on the other side. He would chuck us freshly dug potatoes and promises to take us wild mushroom hunting. This, we discovered later WAS a big deal as they guard the location of those fungi with a passion.

Then there was lovely Griet and Frans. Griet was an artist, gardener and maker of cakes and good coffee. She ran me hot baths when our pipes burst, he mended the pipes. They drove us on a scenic tour of the area when we first arrived and showed us where we could buy tablecloth clips, bin bags and jars of cornichons. I'm telling you that if you ever do embark on this French house malarkey, all you need to do is meet one lot of people like those two and everything will be alright.

Frans was one of the most inventive and interesting men you could ever meet. He was the spit of Van Gogh and I'm not just saying that because he was Dutch. I'm really not that shallow. Or am I? Anyway, he'd been a boxer, a journalist, probably a spy, an engineer, drawn caricatures, cooked for royalty. One of his many jobs had involved being part of a research program on ants, involving him crouching in a field dabbing blue paint on any insect that emerged from the anthill. A gendarme came along, presumed he had escaped from the lunatic asylum down the road and marched him back there pronto.

We loved that little cottage, but one Summer we made the mistake of staying too long. The Limousin is magnificent in many ways, including a marvelous factory shop for dirt cheap Limoges porcelain. But even an infinite supply of delicate, white dishes just wasn't enough to sustain us. One cloudy August morning we cracked, threw a bag in the car and headed South for a change of scene and some golden weather.

Many long hours later, as we rounded the Pyrenees, the sky turned a dazzling sapphire, the earth turned red, the trees turned to cypress, palm and fig. The tacky tarmac ahead wobbled with muscat-sticky heat. We knew we'd reached our El Dorado.

3: CHOCOLAT

"Life is like a box of chocolates. You never know what you're gonna get."

Well, you do really. A load of calories. It's just that some will be more delicious than others. There are the ones everyone fights over and sneaks from the second layer before it's allowed ~ the Turkish Delight, the Truffle, the Coffee Cream. There are the rock hard toffees that have teeth marks in because somebody's tried to have a bite and then put it back. There are the sad ones that always get left behind – Strawberry Creams and Marzipan.

A stone maison de maître with blue shutters, a gravel drive, the tantalizing sparkle of a cool pool across the lawns which are edged in clouds of lavender. An elderly, toothless, dewy eyed couple next door who act as willing – moreover free – guardians in our absence and who proffer pots of rich Daube de Boeuf and freshly baked madeleines on our weary arrival.

My dream holiday house.

This is not that house.

But the budget will dictate. "Let's remember you have to live within your means", "it's all about the exchange rate". These are mantras with which I am familiar lest – heaven forefend – I start to sound ungrateful.

This house is a three story terraced townhouse in a busy working village. We have a little stone courtyard and the neighbors are not dissimilar to the Gallic version of Wayne and Waynetta Slob. Wayne works on the vines and hunts. My husband once knocked on their door and he answered it covered in blood and wielding a huge knife. He was in the process of butchering a wild boar in the kitchen. His wife is the appropriate size to his Jack Spratt and has lungs like Montgolfier's balloon that come in handy when she's bawling at the kids. She swears like a trooper and thinks I can't understand her, but I can and it's done wonders for my vocabulary. The two tiny, emaciated boys are sweet and always smile through snot-drenched fists. I'm sure they've got hearts of gold and would probably bring madeleines if they weren't so partial to takeaway pizza thus circumventing the need to bake.

So the last visit to our holiday home in the Languedoc was like those chocolates. Much anticipated, but a mixture of highs and lows.

On arrival, having thrown open the shutters, ripped the dust covers from the sofa and skipped around the garden pointing out the new growth, The Husband turned on the electricity and water. When I tried to fill the watering can however, there was indeed the sound of gushing but sadly not from the tap. It was coming from the mains pipe. That wasn't good.

It was too late to call a plumber, so we filled up a couple of bottles at a kind neighbor's house and opened a tin of cassoulet and a bottle of wine. After the second bottle I'd almost forgotten how much I wanted a nice hot shower after traveling all day and, the possibility that the leak could be anywhere under the tiled floor and the whole thing might have to be dug up.

The next morning, the village turned off the electricity due to major road works.

This was excellent news, as now we couldn't even boil what was left of our water for a coffee. The only course of action was to adopt the embryonic position under the duvet, while The Husband rang a marvelous man who came toute suite and spent the day fixing a hole in the pipe, which was thankfully accessible - not only to him, but to the mouse that had made it in the first place.

Now, if there is one thing that is more terrifying to us than a foil wrapped Tangerine Cream, it's rodents. We made sure that our own body weight in concrete was thrown down that drain along with a variety of lethal products.

When all was sorted, we breathed a sigh of relief and opened the mailbox in which there was a pile of bills and a court summons for non payment from our ex-Internet provider. I say EX, because we had terminated the contract. I won't name them, but let's just say – The Future was definitely not Bright.

We leapt into the car and steamed down to their shop where there was much jabbing of fingers in faces and heated debate. My husband was actually jabbing his finger in MY face though, as no English was spoken and I was having to translate.

"You tell them that I'm not leaving here until……"

"And you can tell them that I want proof in writing……."

"And what do you MEAN you can't phone the debt collection company? This is a phone shop! Look, there's one! And there's another one….."

Apparently their system hadn't caught up with our instruction to end of the contract. Anyway, it too eventually got sorted.

Back at the house, we took a few moments

to gaze contemplatively at the huge hole in our bedroom ceiling where the plaster had fallen off due to the new terrace above it leaking in the catastrophic rains of November, wishing plaintively that the builder would come and fix the terrace so that the insurance people would come and repair the ceiling and we could move all the furniture back in and actually sleep in the bed without the fear of being rendered dead by an enormous lump of falling plaster.

Oh how we begged that builder to come. How we wandered aimlessly from room to room, found little jobs to distract us, wrote emails to every one who knew him, sent texts until our fingers were numb. Just to make it just a bit more exiting and add a touch of frisson to our dull lives, he waited until our *very* last day to appear and then did a fabulous job.

But it was on one of those listless evenings, sipping an aperitif in the garden that Mr Rigsby announced our French sojourn was just never meant to be like this and, we were selling up. I thought, I know what's needed, a nice dinner to cheer him! Half way through my Poulet au Dijon, the gas canister in the cooker ran out.

In between these dramas there had been a swim in the lake, dinner with friends, a bike ride through the vineyards. As with all Milk Trays, you might not love everything, but once the end has come, you just want more and I can't wait to get back there in a few weeks time when hopefully all will be well.

PS: Going back to chocolates – and why wouldn't you? – we neglected to mention LIQUEURS. In my parent's day, they were considered the height of sophistication. I was allowed, at Xmas, to drain a Crème de Menthe. The Cointreau and Grand Marnier are almost acceptable. I have fiends who have dug them out of a cupboard in desperation when there was no Chardonnay in the house. But, oh dear, Bristol Cream and Malibu……..really? The only time I get them now is as a present from an elderly relative. We all know don't we, when someone offers something up that they think you'll enjoy, it's important to look pleased and grateful, even though you know it might just make you gag and leave a sticky residue running down your chin. So shove them to the back of that cupboard and have a Maltezer and a real drink.

4: THE GUEST LIST

There's no point having all this fabulous weather, countryside, food, wine and general gorgeousness, if you can't spread the love. We couldn't wait for the house to be ready to receive our first guests.

By the time I'd finished with their room it smelt of bees wax and lavender. The bed linen was crisp and fragrant, pillows plumped like big marshmallows. There were sachets of herbs and scented candles, piles of individually wrapped soaps, freshly laundered bathrobes with matching slippers.

I'd provided a little engraved carafe, filled with Muscat and some tiny old glasses from a vide grenier, so they could pour themselves an aperitif. A pile of fluffy towels was neatly folded on the bed, along with a cotton drawstring bag filled with items from various boutique hotels (some might say "nicked", I would say "bought and paid for with the room") - combs, mini shampoos, shower caps, nail files.

On my funny little cooker from Bon Coin, a big pot of chicken in lemon, wild thyme and olives blipped away, filling the kitchen with welcoming aromas of the region.

We'll pick them up from the airport, then we've planned antique hunting, swimming in cool rivers, oysters at the beach. Tomorrow night we'll take them out to that bistro that does the freshest salad Perigueux and the most unctuous cassoulet. After all, they've spent all that money on flights, so we want them to feel welcomed and get a real sense of being in France.

I've got a moleskin notebook that I bought from a papetier in Paris. It can serve as a visitor's book, so they can record their favourite experiences for the benefit of future guests.

A lovely time was had by all and ended in fond hugs and promises of a repeat visit. The house felt very quiet after they'd gone but the next party will be on their way in a few days, so time to get out the Hoover, strip those beds and snip some fresh flowers and olive sprigs, the silvery grey leaves of which, go so well with a mauve hibiscus bloom and some bright pink bougainvillea. A couple of the soaps had been unwrapped and only used once, but no matter. What's an expensive tissue wrapped soap between friends? They certainly had enjoyed the Muscat - well that's what it was there for! - and the loo roll needed replenishing.

Yet another wonderful weekend ensued and more precious memories committed to the moleskin visitor's book. Once again the house felt very quiet when they'd gone.

Quiet, and peaceful.

Restful even.

I imagined the next group of visitors packing and getting excited at the prospect of their weekend away. I thought I'd just send a quick email strongly recommending they hire a car with a Satnav, just so they have that bit of independence, only if they want it. A good hostess should think of everything. I'll leave a pile of maps in their room. Also, I asked if they could just bring a few rolls of toilet paper. I mean, the rate these people go through the stuff! What's wrong with them?

I wonder if I actually need to change the sheets? The last guests were meticulous in their personal hygiene and if I Hoover the bed, who would know? In fact the Hoover is quite a faff to get up the stairs, so maybe an inspection for stray hairs and then a spray with the air freshener from the lav. Similarly, those towels hardly look used, and it's much better for the environment not to do all that washing.

I seem to have drunk the rest of the Muscat while I was doing the last lot of cleaning, so I'll thoughtfully replace it with some tap water in case they get thirsty in the night, and perhaps some paper cups to save on the washing up. I've become quite the Eco-warrior.

There's a Fish and Chips evening at the cafe

tonight. I think they'd enjoy that. I know they can have fish and chips whenever they like in England, but it is a French cafe, they would be drinking French wine and you never know, there might even be a few actual French people there.

And another thing, with all this socialising I'll be in the Betty Ford Clinic by Monday, so maybe they wouldn't mind if I stayed in and watched "Strictly"? I mean, that's one of the signs of an enduring and valued friendship, that everyone can do their own thing and it just doesn't matter. Equally, good friends never outstay their welcome. You never know, they might want to be flexible in their arrangements and leave early. It might cost them a bit extra to change the flights, but they'd offset that by saving a day on the hire car. A considerate hostess thinks of those things.

And that bloody visitor's book can go in the bin. This isn't "Four in a Bed".

...very expensive wrapped soap....

5: HOW NOT TO BE AN ALCOHOLIQUE IN THE LANGUEDOC

It's very easy to slip into the habit of having a glass of wine every night in the Languedoc such is the bounty of land and sea, so beautiful the weather, so lush and green those vineyards in the dipping sun. It's also tempting to have the odd lunchtime tipple if you've got a particularly crusty baguette, a pungent cheese and a bowl of fragrant tomatoes. Or you might be innocently on your way to post a letter and trip over the board advertising the Sport Bar's menu du jour – a crunchy Salad Perigeux, smoky brochettes and the crème brûlée de la maison – 12€ vin compris. If they've gone to all that trouble it's churlish to ignore it and you will be supporting your local community.

Everyone knows that you should have at least three consecutive alcohol-free nights every week.

Monday is easy because it's Monday, so it should be miserable. Beans on buttery toast in front of the telly, with a steaming mug of tea is a lovely change anyway. Tuesday will be easy too, except that it's a gorgeous evening and soon the sun will turn the colour of a squashed Grenache Noir grape and start to stain the blue tablecloth with streaks of rose….and you did buy that huge tub of sticky, yellow paella from the market and it would be an insult to those gambas not to wash it down with a jammy Cabernet.

SO then you won't have anything tomorrow night, which will be alternate nights instead of consecutive, which must be the same thing.

Apero hour is the trickiest time, when you are most likely to succumb as you hear the chink of glass from the neighbour's garden and get a whiff of their tapenade. So here are some diversionary tactics:

1: Identify a remote lake or river and head out for an early evening swim. By the time you get home, have a shower and do your hair you'll be exhausted and can curl up for an early night with an enormous Kate Mosse.

2: Go for a game of tennis. It's the perfect time as it is getting cooler and nothing goes better with tennis than ice cold Robinson's Barley Water, so readily available at the corner Vival. You can follow this with a sanctimonious healthy supper, while watching replays of teetotaler Sir Andy Murray's glorious win of 2013, reassuring yourself that his - and your own - kind of physical perfection doesn't come without sacrifice.

Warning: DO NOT try same tactics with Petanque. It's in the name of the "lo" that the sounds to accompany a game of boules are the clank of metal, the crunch of gravel and the popping of a cork.

3: Visit friends who are genuine, authentic alcoholiques and who will serve you a delicious array of non-alcoholique beverages.

4: Buy your own delicious array of non-alcoholique beverages, like:-

- tangy pineapple juice (the exotic aroma of which just puts you in mind of a Barbados sunset, the hum of the beach bar blending a creamy Piña Colada with that dark syrupy rum)

- refreshing, bitter tonic water clinking with ice cubes (the sort that's just perfect with a spritz of lemon and a drizzle of juniper fragranced Bombay Sapphire)

- or rich tomato juice with a sprinkling of celery salt and shot of Tabasco (which on any other day would so benefit from the acrid background hint of Grey Goose)

5: Buy alcohol free wine and beer.

Hang on a minute, that's ridiculous. It tastes disgusting and is the same as a vegetarian trying to make authentic tasting burgers from a bit of old gravel. It's futile and hypocritical.

Anyway it must be Wednesday by now, which means you've made it to midweek, and if that's not worth celebrating I don't know what is. Then tomorrow's Thirsty Thursday as it's almost the weekend and then it's actually the real weekend and you're home and dry.

Literally.

Well done.

Cheers.

6: NO FLY ZZZONE

A couple of years ago we went to see Jeff Goldblum and Kevin Spacey in "Speed the Plough" at the Old Vic in London Town. It was a balmy Summer's eve and everyone was having a snifter on the pavement in front of the theatre, before curtain up. There I was sipping my chilled white wine when Jeff himself wandered out, cigar in hand, lolloping laconically around, stooping (he's very tall) to shake hands and chat.

In my selective memory, I nattered away in a fascinating manner about his whole oeuvre and Jeff Goldblum – or Jeff Baby as I now feel I can call him – was captivated, inviting me for a nightcap after the show. In reality I stood frozen in awe, mouth gaping, dribbling Chardonnay like some wine soaked simpleton. All I could think about was "The Fly".

I am reminded of that now, because I think I'm taking on fly-like tendencies myself. My proboscis is twitching and I catch myself involuntarily buzzing. I'm constantly swiping madly both at real and imaginary tickles all over my thorax section and abdominal segment. There are SO many of them at certain points in the Summer.

We've heard various theories, like they're brought in by the wind, they come after the sugar in the grapes, it's due to an extra wet Spring or an extra dry Summer. Whatever the reason, I'm verging on the point of inzzzzanity. They settle on your lunchtime baguette, to regurgitate whatever it is they last landed on. Doesn't bear thinking about. They can sense an oyster at 500 feet. When someone leaves a fragment of tapas at the cafe, they are on it like piranhas on a pork chop.

One friend was even considering hanging a side of meat in a corner of the garden as a cunning plan to distract them from the table.

I've got citronella flavoured sticks, candles, nightlights and flares. Nothing works. Yes, you can trap a few with a fly paper, but who wants an unsightly gummy brown strip, studded with wriggling insects, dangling from your tasteful Cannon and Ball painted poutres? There's spray, but who knows what's in that stuff as it drenches your food, enters your orifices and settles on your surfaces?

Someone told me that if you fill a clear plastic bag with water, drop a brass coin in it and hang it in your window, the flies won't come near as they think it's a big beady eye watching them. The trouble is, nobody told the flies. They just thought, what's the silly old bat doing now? and buzzed straight past it in a hum of hysterics.

Well call me old fashioned, but you can't beat a fly swat. We have them in a range of colours and I take one with me wherever I go. I'd actually quite like one of those swishy, horse's tail ones, like Eddy Murphy as that African prince in "Trading Places".

We've also got one of those electric tennis racquet things. But the trouble is you have to make contact first. Anyone looking through the window would think you're having a particularly demented game against Sir Andy Murray on your WI. Having worked up a sweat and smashed a few vases, I decided to just sit motionless on the sofa, waiting for a fly to land on the lethal mesh of its own accord, thumb twitching on the button of death. You should never support electrification unless you're willing to press the button yourself. I was willing, let me tell you, but they always sensed when I was about to unleash the power of an AA battery and escaped before I could fry them. After several days of sitting there, my husband led me slowly, quietly away and hid the implement in a deep, dark place.

I seem to remember that in the original "Fly" movie, there was one with, terrifyingly, a little human face. Imaging that! You're snuggled down in bed, looking forward to an hour with your iPad, the glow of which is so fascinating to an insect. Tapping contentedly away, you hear the tell tale drone. Out of nowhere a sinister black shape lands on your screen to see what you're up to. Slowly it turns its head. A pallid, round human face says in a tiny, squeaky voice, "Ooooh get her! Who doezzz she think SHE izzz writing all that bollockzz. Who wantzzzz to read that!"

Well, you can be sure I'd get that one. SPLAT. Mushed like a raisin in a slice of malt loaf.

So maybe the answer is psychological. Mind over splatter.

I refuse to be driven bonkers by them and let them win. When I'm all creamed up on

my sunbed with a book, a cold drink and a
salted snack, when the first fly lands I'll
ignore it. And the second. I'll laugh
maniacally and, by the time there's twenty
five, I'll employ my Yoga breathing, floating
Zen-like through the itching and bites. After
an hour or so I'll be completely covered from
head to toe in an iridescent, squirming, black
furry coating and all you'll be able to see is a
pair of beady, wild compound eyes.

That's not mad at all! That's perfectly
zzzzane.

Zzzzzz.

Zzz.

Z.

7 FETE DES ETOILES FILANTES

The Perseids. The August meteor showers. A celestial firework display. It seemed as good an excuse as any to have a party!

Being swept along in the festive atmosphere of the Languedoc Summer, even Mr Rigsby was up for the idea. Whereas, if I'd suggested throwing a party back home in The Great Outer London, he'd have changed the subject rapido and locked himself in the shed with his newspaper stapled to his forehead.

But here, it's easy.

Isn't it?

Having a bit of a theme as we did, I zoomed off to the cheap-as-frites shop (plastic flowers, solar frogs, bin ends of paint and knickers in every size). I found a tablecloth and paper plates, all with gold stars on. Gold plastic cups and gold napkins. Rockets and sparklers. Parfait.

Then I thought, this is all very well, but we'd better invite some actual guests or it might seem a bit tragic, just the two of us mingling with one another and forming the world's shortest buffet queue.

I designed the invitation and emailed it out to as many people as I had addresses for. That would be three. Then I asked THEM for a few others, of the people we'd met at THEIR soirees. Then I knocked on a couple of doors. Not of random strangers, you understand. I'm not desperate. Really.

I started planning the food, while the person in charge of potations set out on his mission to find the tastiest vracs in the whole of the Minervois.

SO, big platters is the way to go. I snap them up whenever I see them at vide-greniers. All cold salads - no scalding juices or steam to mess up coiffure, stain frock and cause mascara streaks down red, sweaty face.

Cous cous and roasted vegetables drizzled with Harissa.

Coconut chicken rice in a mould with a hole in the middle for a jaunty sprig of rocket. (Rocket……geddit?)

Mimosa salad – blanched green beans dressed and topped with chopped hard boiled eggs.

Endive, walnut and gorgonzola with a honey dressing.

Watermelon, feta and black olive. (I could have caught a Ryanair back to Waitrose to buy it ready made, in the time it took to deseed that bloody melon.)

Bowls brimming with nuts, crisps and olives.

Piles of crusty baguette.

In a gourmet shop of regional produce, we'd discovered jars of gold – yes, really gold! – truffle mustard. A swish of that on a few pork pate canapés would pass as meteors.

And I bought some of those Flying Saucer sweets, that feel like they're made from polystyrene and decompose on the tongue, depositing fizzy, tooth achy sherbet. And mini MARS bars.

I fleetingly considered making labels for the food, in the shape of the Aurora Borealis or the Hubble Telescope. But life's too short and if people are too stupid to work out what they're eating they should stay in. Especially if they're fussy eaters or they've got food allergies or lactose intolerance or are vegetarians or something. And don't even get me started on Coeliacs.

Some generous guests offered to bring dishes. I suppose one should politely thank them and refuse in a noble and self sacrificial manner. I bit their arms off.

Another friend emailed vis a vis the dress code, which I'd described on the invite as "Out of this World", meaning that it would be a good excuse to glam up. But now I would have sleepless nights in case someone somewhere was slaving over a Pritt Stick, a catering size roll of tin foil and some sticky back plastic. They might wheel themselves in on their knees as R2D2, feel like a complete plonker and need counseling for life. It would all be my fault.

When I found out that one friend was a bit of a crooner, I gently persuaded (press ganged) him into having.........I mean DOING a turn.

On the eve of the event, we spent five hours on a scenic tour of the supermarkets, vegetable stalls and caves of the Herault / Aude / Herault – whatever. My husband said a tearful farewell to a few large denomination notes that he have preferred to have stayed acquainted with. I spent the afternoon having a Close Encounter with my own body weight in Basmati.

Come the day of any gathering, don't you dread the ding dong of an email or the trill of the phone as you assume it's everyone ringing to cancel? No one cancelled. They all turned up in the party mood and dressed to the nines. They were laden with flowers, scrumptious offerings, comet shaped biscuits and a variety of fermented beverages.

The food disappeared; the sparklers sparkled; my "space theme" playlist got the dancing going. When our star turn belted out "Fly Me To The Moon", it brought a tear to the eye. In a good way.

Some of you reading this might even have been there on the night, yet have a different story to tell. You may have found the drinks stingy, the food indigestible and the hostess the worse for wear. You may have been watching the clock and wishing you were on your sofa with "ET" and a gluten free snack.

Well, tough terrestrials. Because it's my party and I'll lie if I want to.

8: PHYSICAL JERKS

Fetes, food and firkins of fine wine make it necessary to perform some manner of physical jerk throughout this over indulgent Languedoc Summer. Heaven forefend I should go back home looking like John Prescott's less body conscious twin.

There was a time when I would have gnawed my own leg off, rather than be seen carrying a yoga mat. But recently I've become enamored with Pilates. It's the kind of exercise I like because it's mainly lying down. It's also fairly sensible. None of this Bing-Bong-Ding-Dong Yoga/Body Balance nonsense. Namaste. Find your inner orifice. You are a dragon flying over the world. Am I? Am I really? I once strayed into such a class with nothing better to do on a wet Saturday afternoon.

It was run by a mad old bat in fuchsia leggings, who skipped around the room scattering battery powered fluorescing mini Buddha's. She spent most of the afternoon saying how she sensed negative vibes coming in her direction. I know she meant they were from me. Actually she was right. Never again.

So before I left for the Summer, a friend dropped off her old yoga mat so that I can continue to practice my Pilates while I remain in the OccitanieMidIMediPairofKnees or whatever they've christened us now. (I mean I like an Occitaine product as much as the next person – their Green Tea and Jasmine eau de toilette is a winner – but it's so complicated and quite exhausting trying to remember all those names.)

Anyway, where was I? Oh yes, looking up my downward dog. I shall perform my contortions in the privacy of my own home. To do it in a public arena would be a grave mistake. Setting up on a beach or in the park and starting to contract my core would be wholly inappropriate and somewhat attention seeking, like those people on Instagram who only ever post pictures of themselves balancing with one foot in their ear in a picturesque setting. What's wrong with them?

I'll let you know how the self inflicted Pilates goes, but it might need some back up in the form of actual moving about and panting.

Here are my options:

Running – So I'll leap out of bed, don my trainers and bind myself in Spandex. Raring to go, I'll make a quick coffee first, because the caffeine will help get me up to full speed. Actually, there might be an almond croissant to go with that, just for my energy levels. I don't want to have a queer turn in the middle of the vineyard. Who would ever find me?

I might check a few emails while I'm having my power breakfast. Have you noticed how time just gets swallowed up once you switch on that iPad? A couple of hours will just race by……messages……the news……today's edition of Languedoc Living……the digital Hello magazine…….a quick game of Scrabble. Before you know it, the bells will be going bonkers for noon, which means, sadly, that the sun is at its zenith and you'd have to be both mad and an Englishwoman to go running in that heat. Anyway it's lunchtime.

Playing Tennis – There are some lovely courts in the park, we have bats (circa 1987, but they'll do the job. What's wrong with wood anyway?) and some downy balls. I am an avid Wimbledon fan and therefore practically a professional….but….who am I going to play with? Absolutely NOT the husband. There lies arguments and days of sulking. Why would someone start doing those tricky, spinney shots and hit the ball to places where they know you can't hit it back? Where's the fun in that? I don't actually know anyone else though, so tennis is out.

Cycling – At every vide grenier we snap up those old bikes. We have a variety for when visitors come, that's the idea anyway. They are in various states of repair, style and size. The trouble is that none of them are MY size, except one that used to be a circus bike for Coco the Clown. The handlebars turn backwards and the wheels go in opposite directions. And don't even talk to me about what the saddle does to one's posterior parts over the rough terrain of a canal side path.

Swimming – YES, this is it! A serene stretch of lake, the mountains in the distance, cool, clear water. There's a reason though, why our lake is a hotbed for windsurfers. The clue's in the name…..wind. Being slapped full in the face with a wet mackerel could be relatively pleasant on occasion, but ten times per minute isn't what you'd call enjoyable.

That's the sensation you get when you're battling against the waves, a force ten in your face. It's like swimming the Atlantic in a hurricane. Cutting sleekly through the chop like Sharon Davies would be ideal, but spluttering and gasping towards that buoy in the distance bears no resemblance. That big, round old buoy, it bobs on the water like my own Mr Rigsby's lovely, shiny bald head, waiting for me to cling desperately on for dear life, before mounting the assault on the return trip.

Then there's the getting out! Everyone sitting by the side of that lake is facing you. No matter that that some are engaged in their children, absorbed by their book, fascinated by their feet, they're all still FACING you. So I emerge from the surf like Ursula Andress in Dr No. If Ursula Andress had hair plastered to her face, was grasping her Primark pants because the elasticity isn't what it used to be, if she is grimacing like a gargoyle because of the excruciating pain of the pebbles digging into the pallid soles of her hairy feet, squinting around in vain for wherever the hell she left her flip flops, then yes , I do look just like her. It's uncanny.

So I think all in all it's back to the Pilates. I'll

find a nice, sane looking woman on You Tube that I can follow, settle on a cool spot in the house, become prone and while I'm down there I might take a short nap and a Bourbon biscuit. Well you don't want to overdo it. You don't get a body like this by rushing into things, I can tell you.

9: LETTING GO

When we pop over to the Languedoc for a week or two, we fly courtesy of Mr Michael O'Ver-your-luggage-allowance, who permits me to bring one pair of pants and a handkerchief. So, when we are planning a longer sojourn and therefore driving, I get very excited about the capaciousness of a car boot. It ALL goes in:

Vests, tops and T-shirts – long sleeved for chilly evenings, short sleeved for when bingo wings are tanned (rendering them invisible), large for covering bottom, stretchy for covering everything else.

Dresses – long and floaty for Isadora Duncan moments, short for fooling myself I can still get away with it.

Skirts – short (see above), ankle length, mid length……..all areas covered. A trouser and a tight – you have to consider every eventuality. Knickers for all occasions, bras, bikinis, sarongs, wraps, scarves, shawls, peshwari nans.

Bags, baskets, clutches and rucksacks, oh and the shoes…….high heeled, kitten heeled, wedges, flats, flip flops. Those for walking in, those impossible to walk in, leopard skin, sparkly, shiny and sequined.

I do a Supermarket Sweep of Wilkinson's and pack lotions and potions into every orifice. Of the car. Sun stuff, hair stuff, skin stuff, smelly stuff, more stuff in case the other stuff runs out.

When we arrive at the house, after fighting through the cobwebs and when the dusters and bleach have been put away, I unpack it all into the enormous wardrobe that had to come in through the bedroom window, with the brocanteur balancing on the kitchen roof. I fill drawers, baskets, tastefully sourced boxes and cartons.

And there it all stays until the day we leave.

The truth of the matter is, that after a few days here I sink into a style stupor, a fashion flop, a costume coma. Maybe it's the heat, the pace of life, or the three bottles of wine with dinner – I don't know. But it's really as much as I can do to drag one leg after the other in to a pair of bikini bottoms. For a visit to the shops, for the sake of decency I'll pull on a crumpled, comfy frock, probably stained from yesterday's gazpacho and some flaccid flip flops.

For a night out I do make a bit more effort, it's true. An almost clean, loose dress that won't show the VPL, bulging more with each dish of cassoulet. I might even risk a smear of red lipstick and then I look like a film star!

Not so much Scarlett Johansen. I'm thinking more Heath Ledger as the Joker in Batman.

Well, make up just melts off you doesn't it? Mascara ends up like Alice Cooper watching "Titanic".

And who wants to sit there sweating and grappling with a hair dryer for half an hour, when it eats into precious apero time? A comb through with a bit of lard and we're good to go. As for depilatory cream……fuggedaboudit.

My girlfriends at home would be horrified that I've let myself go in this way. They've got this vision of me prancing round in the South of France in black a linen Jigsaw sundress one minute, a crisp Zara Breton top and white shorts the next. They must never know the truth.

The final stage will be that one day I'll just go down to the market and buy a nylon housecoat with a pair of fluffy slippers and live in those. The husband can purchase some of the ubiquitous blue overalls and a cloth cap. (He's Northern so will probably feel quite at home anyway.) Then neither of us will have to bother getting either dressed or undressed ever again. I can shuffle along the road, pause on street corners to look bewildered for a while and then shuffle back again. It will save an awful lot of time and money and I'll never have to smuggle extra clothes (by wearing multiple layers) past Mr O'Ver-Ten-Kilos again.

10: LA VIE EN ROSE

Early one morning, we received an email from a wine-maker friend:

"We've decided to start the vendange today. If you are free to help this morning, come and find us in the vines."

How exciting. The final piece of the puzzle. A house in the Languedoc, bills from EDF, a baguette drawer, our own well – and now we were going to be an integral part of the heritage of the area. Grape picking for our vigneron friends. It just doesn't get more French.

The first and most obvious question was, what to wear? Should I be channeling

Huckleberry Finn – a pair of washed out denim dungarees with a jaunty spotted neckerchief? How about a long, cool dress that would waft around in the fruit scented breeze?

No, I think I'll opt for a cotton print skirt, with pockets for my vintner's equipment and mascara. A hand, casually looped in one pocket says……I've turned up here to help, but I'm not desperate or anything. A spotless T-shirt and a rather stylish straw hat from the market, which hails originally from Australia – a nod to the Hunter Valley. A nice touch I thought.

I did consider a heel, but in the end went for new grey pumps with bright white soles and matching laces – practical, yet not in a George Sand sort of a way.

I think Chanel Rouge Absolut lipstick would be a bit much here, even for me. A MAC lip gloss? Very sticky, might attract flies. I could pop into my poche just in case. Now, how to do my hair……

All that sorted, two hours later we parked up outside their house. I knew that their vineyard was behind it, but just to check I asked a neighbour, who pointed to the left:

"Oui, la-bas. C'est pas loin a pied."

So we set off, me swinging my matching basket, filled with essentials for the professional grape picker like water, camera, perfume, phone, spare sunglasses.

After one and a half hours, not having seen a soul, we stomped back again, bickering. Obviously I blamed my husband for faffing around at home, making us late. Now my morning, my day, actually probably my whole life was ruined, as we had missed out on the grape picking experience.

Then up roared our friend in a bright orange mini moke and an even brighter grin. "Oh here you are! Just in time for lunch."

We sat on a shaded terrace around a long table with our fellow workers. Well alright, I know we hadn't actually done any work, but still we felt the camaraderie, the bonhomie. Anyone could tell I was one of them. Accepted and fully integrated. We threw ourselves into the banter.
"Biensur…..d'accord……donc…..mange tout Rodney….."

Plump chunks of pink Pate de
Campagne accompanied by glistening
cornichons were followed by a hearty pork
stew. Some coffee (small, strong and black
of course) – and then "Allons- y".

We all bundled into jeeps, tractors and
trucks and headed off in bumpy convoy, in a
direction that was diametrically opposed to
that pointed out earlier by the neighbour.

At the end of a row of vines, clutching a pair
of secateurs and a bucket, we listened
intently to instructions. Leave the little
grapions, cut just above the fruit, no foliage
and leap frog each other down the row. How
fabulous, I thought, that despite the
seriousness of the task they still found time
for recreation. I hadn't played leap frog in
years and gave a silent prayer of thanks that
I'd put on a sturdy pair of pants.

I soon realised however that it actually
meant, keep passing the picker in front of
you. Never mind. Here we go then, I am now
a true Langedoccian, indispensable to the
process of creating this Syrah.

Snip, pick, drop, snip (oops another
fingernail gone), pick, drop.

Disconcertingly another, more proficient
picker would occasionally attack my vine
violently from the other side. A flash of blade
and a flurry of leaf by Edward Scissorhands,
and I was fearful for my digits. I ran ahead a
few bushes and hid until he or she decided
to go and pick on somebody else.

Snip, pick, drop, snip, pick, drop.

Back at home hours later, exhausted but
with a huge sense of satisfaction and
accomplishment, I happened to pass by a
mirror. We seemed to have an intruder!

This person had on a weird bushwhacker
type hat. Any visible hair was plastered
down flat and dripping with sweat. Her face
was bright pink and – good god – were those
flies stuck to her lips? Her T- Shirt was
stained with sweat and purple juice. Her legs
were bloody and scratched, ankles covered
in a fine brown dust. Her pockets seemed to
be inexplicable stuffed with cosmetics and it
looked like she'd been given a manicure by
Stevie Wonder. Some filthy grey shoes were
splattered in something looking suspiciously
like sanglier excrement. She was clutching a
misshapen basket that had tractor tyre
marks all over it."Thank goodness I don't

look like her!" I thought, bounding up the stairs. I say bounding, actually hobbling with a crooked spine, as the backache was starting to kick in. Under a steaming hot shower, dousing myself in, what else but Occitaine shower gel, I scrubbed the grit and foliage out of my Audrey Tatou locks and sighed, "La Gloire de Mon Hair".

We were now fully accepted as part of the vigneron community. We had broken bread together – "Le Pain Quotidian". We'd shared a bonding experience and we had French blood running through our veins like Malbec through a tablecloth.

I stumbled back downstairs, had beans on toast with a mug of tea, and fell asleep in front of "Coronation Street."

Aaahhh, la vie en rosé.

11: TOTALLY FETED

I had a culturally enlightening evening with a French friend at our local bar recently. She was instructing me in the various brightly, some might say garishly, coloured drinks that one longs to try but are too scared to ask for. I am officially classified as a Practical Learner, so her telling me about it wouldn't have been enough. I had to actually see a demonstration. So, we started with Le Mauresque.

This is Pastis with a dash of Almond Syrup. It takes the harsh edge off the Pastis and lends it a slightly sweeter tone. HOW sweet depends on the generosity of the pourer. Mauresque means "Moorish" – like Othello – not because of the fact that you could quite easily just keep having more.

By the way, the phrase "oooh it's really moreish", for me, should be confined into the same verbal trash can as the word "impact" being used as a verb. But that's just mwah.

Anyway, on to my second cultural investigation, which was Pastis with a dash of Crème de Menthe. This lends the drink an obvious mint note and turns it a vivid green, putting one in mind of either The Hulk after a minibreak to Dungeness, or the exotic plumage of the parrot, Le Perroquet, after which it's named.

The finale of the evening was a Tomate – a Pastis with a shot of Grenadine. The taste, originating from pomegranate juice, is both sweet and tart. The colour, that of a perfectly ripe beef tomato. This can be a bit tricky to order, as you could catch your server on bad day and he/she might actually plonk down a perfectly ripe beef tomato. My friend advised asking for a Tomate Pastis just to be on the safe side.

Other possibilities and the Higher National Diploma of my instruction, are:

Rourou: made with strawberry syrup and,

Feuille Mort (the appetizingly named "dead leaf"): made with grenadine and green mint syrup.

A number of additional culturally fascinating facts emerged, by way of a Hidden Curriculum. Most of these seem to have escaped memory for some reason, but one

I do remember is the poignantly and succinctly put:

"*When it comes to the start of July it's really difficult to organise anything because everyone is off all over the place doing something and everything and that and stuff. One for the road?*"

Yes, I get it. And I'm feeling the effects right now.

I'm emotionally and physically drained.

I'm totally feted.

I'm fete for nothing.

If it's not the fete of the olive, it's the fete of the garlic, melon or apricot. There are village fetes which last for days and involve propping up wine barrels in the street and listening to brain splitting music. There are those ones which involve hare arsing around after bulls and those ubiquitous Brazilian Dancers.

Every weekend there are umpteen vide greniers. You see the signs written in felt pen tied to a wonky stick alongside one of the faster D roads, or in the middle of a hugely busy roundabout. When you've driven round six times in order to be able to read It without stopping, you barrel off in the direction of that village – and there – all the signs stop.

Then it's like that scene out of "It's a Mad, Mad, Mad, Mad World", when Phil Silvers and co: are all looking for the Big W.

Cars all congregate at the meeting of a cross roads, everyone eyes each other suspiciously, then they tear off in different directions before meeting up again at a crossroads on the other side of town. Eventually everyone ends up following some poor, random passerby and, when the actual event has finally been spotted, they race to a parking spot and leg it to those stalls lest anyone should snap up their bargain. After all, hasn't everyone come looking for a bright orange, plastic potato ricer with an Eiffel Tower logo? Well if they have, I'M getting it first.

There are concerts, dances, recitals. There are boules matches, tennis tournaments, lotto, picnics and fireworks. There are gigantic cauldrons of Paella, seiche, moules and escargots all bubbling over smouldering vines. Any excuse to set up a trestle table and they're there.

I can be sitting in the peace and quiet of my little courtyard practicing my yoga breathing and, a blast of deafening music will come from nowhere, causing me to spit Earl Grey all over my new Primark holiday top. This is followed by the barely intelligible, echoey, disembodied voice. "ALLO ALLO." When it's

not telling me to give my blood, pick up my
poubelle bags or move my car, I am being
ordered to attend the local community
centre for a poetry recital, soup making
competition, art show opening or just a
general knees up.

There was a "Marché Artisanal Nocturne" the
other night. This sounded promisingly
civilized and restrained. We'd been invited
for an apero first, so the whole evening was
shaping up to be sophisticated and
intellectually diverse. Well, the apero started
with champagne and ended with shrieking
over delicious chicken curry, after which we
staggered out to the covered market to
peruse a misshapen bar of soap, a jar of fig
preserve, a carefully crafted lavender sack.
Blow me, if there wasn't a ring of trestle
tables, a gigantic BBQ, a demented DJ and
people hurling themselves around doing Le
Jive as if their lives depended on it.

The spitting, charcoaled duck looked too
good to miss out on and they'd gone to all
that trouble......so we had a second dinner
and ended up popping bottles of Blanquette
de Limoux with a lovely French couple we'd
never set eyes on before in our lives. We
tottered home at 2am and I blame them for

everything.

It's not even confined to weekends.

We cycled over to a gorgeous fete on the banks of a canal, with coloured lights illuminating the trees and water. There were people in deckchairs listening to music through enormous headphones. There was restauration – a garlicky seiche in rouille sauce and a nougat glacé. There were people, of course, propping up wine barrels and laughing their heads off. There were choirs, animateurs and holiday boaters having elaborate dinners on candlelit decks.

And it was a Tuesday!

Back in Blighty, Tuesday nights are for balancing beans on toast on your knee and catching up with Holby City.

I mean, what's with all this joie de vivre, enjoyment and bonhomie anyway? Why can't people be bored, miserable and unfriendly like we are back in Suburban London? What's wrong with everyone?

The trouble is, it's infectious.

We are going to have an actual party!

If I uttered the words "Let's have a party" at home in the UK, Mr Rigsby's nose would be so firmly stuck inside his Guardian, you'd need pliers to get it out. But here, oh no, it's straight off to the shop that sells paper plates and fireworks, canapé planning and a mission to find the best deal on vracs of red.

This Languedoc Living just can't go on. It's unsustainable and thank goodness that there's only a month until September when it will all wind down.

Well…..apart from the fact that SOMEONE'S got to celebrate the pumpkin, the wild mushroom and the chestnut or they might be offended. And then of course, there's the Vendange and all those grape picking lunches and fetes to welcome the first wine………..

Oh, fete it! Let's get stuck in.

12: TO MISS AND BE MISSED IN THE LANGUEDOC

When you are away for home for long spells, however lucky you are to spend time in a beautiful place like this, there will be things you miss. Most importantly, family and friends. But thanks to broadband, smartphones and tablets, communication is easy. Therefore, meaningful and informative conversations, via messaging systems with loved ones is entirely possible.

With my son.

"Hello darling. How are you? We miss you. Having a lovely time here, Dad is so relaxed. We're eating and drinking far too much. Ha ha. LOL."

"Yh."

"So how are you? How's work? I hope everything is going well. Do tell us all the news and how it's all going? Is everything fine?"

"OK."

"That's lovely to hear. We miss you too. And

is Granddad well, and your sister?"

"There's no bog roll."

"Sorry darling. Did you just say there's no loo roll? It's just that we are over here in France and you're over there in England at home, so there's not actually much we can do about that is there? LOL."

"You're really p****** me off now. There's no point talking to you when you're like this. I'm going."

"OK darling, well it was lovely to chat. Love you. Miss you."

Conversation over.

With my daughter.

"Hi darling. How are you?"

"Mum, I'm so stressed, because Dipsie was a real pain last night. It's all about her and she never asks how I am. OMG she's so selfish. I know she's my best friend but I don't think I want to see her again. And that dress I just ordered from ASOS doesn't fit, so it's got to go back and I've got nothing to wear to Dipsie's party tonight. There's no loo roll. And your precious son's being so annoying and he ate my chicken nuggets, so I've had nothing to eat for 3 days because you didn't leave enough food."

"That's a shame darling, I'll have a word with him. But Dad and I are having a lovely time

thanks. He's very relaxed and we're working hard on the house, making your room nice for you!"

"Oh and I got another parking ticket, it's so unfair, and it's not my fault because Dipsie parked there last week. So, love you, love you, I've got no money. So can you send me some because everyone else will have a new dress for tonight except me. Love you. Did I say there's no loo roll?"

"Sorry, darling, I don't think we can give you any more money and it couldn't be there by tonight anyway. Maybe if you'd spent the last lot we sent on food and loo roll? Ha ha! LOL."

"OMG that's so selfish."

Conversation over.

Aaaahh and there's my dear old dad. Deaf as a post, but bound to be missing me madly too. The trouble is that he can't work the phone I got him, or the Internet in general, so communication has to be via my husband's mobile phone. The one that he keeps switched off because of roaming charges.....

"Hi Dad! It's me. How are you?"

(Loud crackling sound) "Sorry, who is this?"

"It's me again Dad, from France."

"You're going to a dance? That's lovely darling. Are you popping down today?"

"No dad, I'm in France, at the house! Remember? I told you yesterday"Hang on a minute....do you know what.....this hearing aid's getting worse. Maybe if I........"

(Loud whistling noises)

Meanwhile, Mr Rigsby is hopping from one foot to the other, jabbing his watch with his finger and turning the colour of a ten euro note.

"Better go now Dad, it's quite dear from here."

"You fancy a beer? That's not like you. Still,

maybe when you pop down later. Do you know what……..this phone isn't working properly. Let me just……"

Whirr. Buzz. Click.

Conversation over.

Sod the lot of them. I'm off to the bar.

13: A PROPOS APERO

So we are now some of the half and half variety of "Languedoc Livers". We have one leg in, one leg out of the pantalon of French life. We straddle the channel. We are Bobby-Both-Ways. Go either way for a toffee apple. So a few things still remain a mystery. We have made various friends nearby and, as fabulous and funny as they are, there is something that a few of them just don't get.

Apero.

We invite them for apero and they turn up at

9.00pm.

"Oh, we thought you'd have eaten by now. We were waiting til you'd finished eating."

Well, we hadn't finished eating. We hadn't even started, because we were waiting to you to come for a drink before we ate. Now I won't get any dinner and I'll be drinking on an empty stomach and be hugging the porcelain at 3.am.

So we tried inviting them out for an aperitif.

"We'll meet you at 6.30 at that bar then."

"Ok, great, there might be music on there later. So we'll grab a bite first. Do you want to join us?"

No. NO. NOOOOOO.

So for them and anyone else similarly unenlightened, here is an apero guide.

1) WHAT IT IS

Aperitif means "something sipped before a meal", deriving from the Latin, aperire, "to unlock or open". It's a drink intended therefore, to "open up" the appetite, to whet or stimulate it. It's usually accompanied by a gouter, or snack, and occurs roughly between 6.00 and 8.30 in the evening. If you are enjoying the buzz and conviviality at your local bar, happen to nip to the loo round about 8.00ish, come out expecting the nods and winks of sociable familiarity – you will in fact be Norman-No-Mates as everyone will have made a run for it to eat their dinner. It wasn't something you said.

The French also regard this time as a punctuation mark between the busy working day and the evening, a sociable and convivial prelude to the ceremony of a leisurely dinner.

2) WHAT TO DRINK

You might think that a can of cider and a BBQ Pringle is the height of sophistication, but now we are virtually French, standards and Duralex glasses must be raised.

A suitable aperitif is a light, averagely alcoholic beverage, meant to ignite the appetite without numbing the senses, or taste buds. Therefore hard liquor is not usually offered. (Having said that, what finer words are there than, "I'm making Cosmos.")

It might just be a glass of flinty Picpoul de Pinet or Champagne. Perhaps a Kir, with blackcurrant, blackberry, chestnut, violet, peach or raspberry liqueur, first invented in Burgundy in the 1940s, by Félix Kir. He was a hero of the Resistance during the Second World War and afterwards, the Mayor of Dijon. Canon Kir, being a typical Frenchman, was a loyal and passionate supporter of Dijonnais products, including the local peasant white wine. However, it was highly acidic, so he added sweet Crème de Cassis to make it more palatable.

But there are all sorts of other exciting aperitifs to discover – Lillet, Floc de Garonne, Ricard, Dubonnet, Suze, Noilly Prat (pronounce it as you see it), Aperol, Campari, Pineau de Charentes, Byrrh. These kinds of aromatic concoctions are often mixed from antiquated, secret herbal recipes and sometimes only available in the village from which they originate.

A small beer is acceptable. There was a very funny article in the Times by a well known raconteur that some might say is a bit of a nob. But he adroitly pointed out ways to recognise British men in a French bar. For example, they are the ones guzzling back pints, as they just don't regard it butch enough to drink beer in the smaller glasses favoured by their Gallic counterparts, who are comfortable enough with their own sexuality not to care. Which is why they also carry man bags.

3) WHAT TO EAT

Sour, salty, smoky, spicy are all flavours that complement aperitifs – olives, nuts, pretzels, saucisson. But if you want to show off and do an "apero dinatoire", which is a bit more elaborate, here are a few ideas. Get a grip though – don't get too carried away. By the time you've fiddled around with your own body weight in canapés, and been up all night wildly spearing satay sticks like a demented Zorro, for the same money and time you could have laid on a four course dinner and be done with it.

Dips

Before serving dips you must make an assertive announcement about double dipping. Double dipping cannot be tolerated in a civilized society. No one should ever have to chew on someone else's corner-mouth droppings. What if your guests have over active saliva glands? Beards? Colds? What if they are just stomach churningly ugly? If you don't feel able to implement this rule, only serve solid food. Otherwise try these…….

Cannellini beans mushed up with lots of olive oil, lemon juice and garlic.

Peas puréed with plain yogurt, parmesan and mint.

Roasted aubergine flesh pulped with Harissa, olive oil and garlic.

Philly & chilli – cream cheese drizzled with sweet chilli sauce.

For an easy hot fondue, bake a whole Camembert stuck with garlic cloves and rosemary sprigs.

The cocktail stick is the apero host's best friend. It's also a very pleasing combination of consonants. Try it!

CoCKKKK-Tail-STiCKKK.

Roll it round your tongue. Not literally obviously or you'll loose a filling or end up looking like that bloke in "Hellraiser". They are a brilliant invention and reasonable priced, having multiple purposes – you can use them for toothpicks, manicures and sticking into the soft parts of guests you don't like much, then innocently looking in the other direction. It is intensely irritating though, when people (men) don't put the top on the box properly and you have to play mini "Pick Up Sticks" at the bottom of your kitchen cupboard.

Things to put on cocktail sticks

All items to be cut into bite size chunks obviously. For example, mozzarella. A whole one per stick would be costly and difficult to get in your mouth in one go, whilst maintaining an elusive air of sophistication.

Mozzarella, basil leaf, cherry tomato. (Colours of the Italian flag/Xmas.)

Cantaloupe melon and a mint leaf wrapped in prosciutto.

Feta and watermelon.

Figs wrapped in prosciutto, baked until the fig goes sweet and gooey, the ham salty and crisp.

Canapés

The olive man on the market sells bags of
golden, crunchy ready baked baguette
rounds, if life is too short to do it your self.
Smother them in combinations of…….

Soft chevre and fig chutney

Humus and Harissa

Pate and cornichon

Guacamole and crème fraiche

Gorgonzola and honey

Sour cream and salmon roe

Sun dried tomato paste and feta

Plump, salty oysters are always welcome and
come packaged in their own handy dishes,
over which to drizzle shallot vinegar and
Tabasco. Baked asparagus sticks, wrapped in
Parma ham, sprinkled with Parmesan go
down well, as do iced shot glasses of
Gazpacho, lightly laced with vodka. A chum
recently presented me with a beetroot
version. Now personally, I would rather
gnaw my own leg off than eat beetroot, but
the colour was fabulous and I'm told it was
delicious if you like that kind of thing.

4) WHAT TO DO AFTER APERO

A much admired friend, a role model really, told me that she recently had to stagger back from an apero party, lie down on the sofa and eat a family size bag of Maltezers. I can't think of any way to top that, so I recommend that's what everybody does.

Well, it's coming up to 6.30, so must dash. I've got an appointment with a vrac of co-op wine and a bag of Hoola Hoops. So next time I invite you – GET IT RIGHT. I have a cocktail stick and I'm not afraid to use it.

14: BALLS OF STEEL

There is a beautiful park in our village. It's an oasis of peace and quiet save for the cacophony of quacking from some ducks who jostle with the terrapins for the best sunbaked rock. Swans slide across the pond and bamboo creaks in the breeze. There are rose arbours and velvet lawns, the plink plonk of tennis balls and the murmur of toddlers playing in the sand.

Deep in the centre of it all, a group of gentlemen rendezvous each and every afternoon. They are so familiar, that they mirror one another's attitudes of ease and relaxation on the green iron benches and scattered chairs. Their jackets, muted colours of tweed and gabardine, dangle from wire pegs on the fence. Their caps remain firmly on their heads.

As they chat amicably, discussing politics, the weather and the state of the vines, they play pétanque. It's a leisurely affair, run through with a serious streak of competition. There is a knowing manner to the polishing of their well worn spheres of grey and silver, which clank together as they thud on the grit, spitting gravel.

One late and languid Summer's afternoon, five friends and I decided to join them on an adjacent pitch. We were unsure of how we'd be received, not wanting to intrude on their revered tradition. However they were accepting, if bemused at our arrival in a flurry of pastel colours, picnic baskets, boules and bottles.

This is how it went…..

"When shall we have the picnic?"

"Now."

"We've only just arrived!"

"In ten minutes then."

"Salmon is the classic sandwich."

"No it's not – it's cucumber, but it's got to be brown bread."

"No it hasn't. White. With mayonnaise."

"NO! Salad cream."

"Is it too early for wine?"

"Who's on what team? Couples can't play together. It's a recipe for disaster."

"We'll pick like we did in PE at school at school."

"No I'm not playing with you."

"Well I never wanted to play with you anyway."

(I've noticed that the French gentlemen have paused their game and are gazing at us with wry, amicable smiles.)

"How do you play anyway? You never said you were in a club. That's not fair."

"It is fair. It was ages ago."

"It's not fair."

"It is fair."

"Everyone has to hold 2 boules. I want the shiny ones."

"No I want the shiny ones."

"I've got the ones with lines on."

"I wanted those ones. You have the criss crossed ones."

"Mine don't match. She's got one of mine. Give it back."

"She's standing over the line!"

"Why is he crouching in that weird position? Is that allowed?"

"Is it over arm or under arm?"

"You hit mine out the way. That's cheating,"

"Shut up."

(One of the previously benign gentlemen appears to be looking at us a little more fixedly now. You might even say……..menacingly……..as if trying to weigh up whether he could take us all out in one fling of a missile, in the manner of ten pin bowling.)

"Those ducks are getting on my wick."

"What's the score? No, that's wrong."

"Mine's closest to the pig."

"No it's not. Mine is."

"Well you can't tell whose is who's because everyone took the wrong boules."

"Well, I did say………"

"Use a bit of string."

"We haven't got string. Use that stick."

"We've run out of wine."

(The gentlemen have left.)

"We've won. LOOOOOOOOsers!"

"Best of three."

"We've still won."

"No you haven't. That didn't count."

"Yes it did."

"Eat gravel, losers. Same time next week?"

14: INDIGESTIBLE INSIDES

"Let's eat out."

Words to get one mentally punching the air.
The hints have been dropped...
"Wasn't the duck lovely at that place.
Anyway, we've got a healthy green salad.
And by the way we're out of wine. But it
doesn't matter."
Showers, shoes and perfume. An excuse to
change out of your bikini and comfy skirt. A
picture comes to mind of a rustic courtyard,
gravel underfoot, chestnut leaves above. An

old, iron bistro table flecked with jasmine petals. A vivid bougainvillea studded with twinkling lights.

First and foremost, LIGHTING. Lighting is key to any interior. Fluorescent lights which cast a green pallor on your partner and the food are just not inviting. Either that, or the Herr Flick spotlight directed straight into your eye, causing an unattractive squinting action and temporary blindness.
May I suggest a dimmer switch, a very simple solution and a relatively cheap one-off investment? A huge bag of night lights from your local euro shop or nearest Scandinavian purveyor is also relatively inexpensive and makes such a difference to the ambiance. No need to purchase candle holders, just collect lovely little jars and interesting tins with gorgeous graphics on the side – the sort that olives, tapenade, sea salt and fig chutney come in. I guarantee that the punters will stay half an hour longer and therefore spend those few euros more, so reluctant will they be to tear themselves away from the cosy flicker.

Talking of which, so many restaurants have amazing fireplaces, which sit dark and dismally empty. It only takes one little log to create a welcoming glow and a musky smoke scent. Yes – even in the summer. I'm sure I read once that Terence Conran, in his beautiful house in Provence, gets his staff to light a roaring log fire every night of the year whether he is staying there or not. I find this an admirable piece of lifestyle ethos, to which I aspire.

Next, COLOUR, the very flesh of design. What's with all the vivid terracotta – or what I call, orange. Orange, red and yellow are all colours that stimulate the brain, get you going. They are used by interior designers in places where they don't want you to hang around and sit still. In a bedroom they keep you awake. In other words, they get me rushing through my menu du jour faster than a chocolate finger at Weightwatchers.

Similarly we have the very ill advised use of pastel blue, often depressingly rag-rolled or even more upsetting, sponged. It's no doubt intended to be reminiscent of a Languedoc Summer sky and it can make a space feel larger than it is. But blue is an appetite suppressant. With the exception of the occasional berry, there is no blue food. Subliminally, we associate blue with rot, decay, and poison. Experiments have actually been carried out with blue food and diet control. Nobody touched the stuff they dyed blue.

Stick to neutrals with accent colours. This means that you can introduce a bit of butternut amber, grapey purple, cornichon green, even a buttery yellow – but in a napkin or pepper pot. Don't hit us over the head with a whole wall of it. Of course Farrow and Ball – (or Cannon and Ball as my husband insists on calling them. I married beneath me) – produces a palette of marvelous greys and taupes with fabulous names like "Hippo's Halitosis" and "Sewage Pipe". They are however, outrageously expensive. Similar tones can be matched and mixed at a fraction of the price.

Finally, ART. The connection between food and art is undeniable and joyous. However if you are one of those people who "know nothing about art but know what you like" please keep it to yourself because we won't. Especially when we're eating. Nothing turns the stomach more that an impasto rendition of a terrifying clown. Particularly if he's crying in an ironically poignant fashion. Frolicking kittens have the same effect, especially when painted in fluorescent colours on black velvet.

Photography is a bit safer, although when I am consuming the bounty of a beautiful local terrain, why would I want to eat in front of an enormous photo of the Brooklyn Bridge? The real one YES please. The River Cafe in New York is one of the things that makes life worth living. But here, let's celebrate these olive groves, vineyards, mountains and seascapes.

(BTW, artistic arrangements of ostrich feathers and glass beads do not belong on a dinner table as they look like they've just dropped off a Burlesque performer's pants. A few wild flowers or a rosemary sprig in a jam jar would be so much nicer. Feathers and food....it's just wrong.)

If you restaurateurs are still in any doubt, please call me. I would be happy to come and help, not in a Laurence Llewellyn Bowen "reduce you to tears with a puce makeover" sort of way, but I could provide a few helpful tips. And then I'm sure you'd be equally as happy to tell me where to shove them, before getting back to what you do best, cooking my delicious dinner. Now where's my lipstick.

THINGS TO DO, PLACES TO GO:

CARCASSONNE – TAPAS & TORTURE

The scent of honeysuckle is being stifled by that of wood smoke. The amber melons at the market are squashed by bright orange pumpkins and the crunch of gravel on the boules pitch is overlaid by a crackle of desiccated leaves. It's a good time to visit Carcassonne – with less chance of being trampled by hordes in aubergine hued shell suits.

What is it with tourists? They go to visit a beautiful city or historical monument, grab a lovely lunch, do a bit of shopping, meander around a gallery or a park and dress as if they are mounting an assault on Annapurna. Trainers, tracksuits, climbing boots, rucksacks, fleeces and that most unattractive of accessories, the visual aberration that is the bum bag. All dress sense leaves them. And selfie-sticks? We know where we'd all like to shove those.

We booked into the Hotel Montmorency, the sister establishment to Hotel du Chateau which is posher and more expensive. But it's just over the road and shares the same reception. Best of all you can use Hotel du Chateau's pool, spa and chic bar, which has a fabulous view of the walls of La Cite, being right opposite. It's a prime spot for an aperitif.

The parking was €10 per day, but easy and secure, so worth it I'd say. You can park up and forget about the car. We had a coffee in the bar while we waited for the room to be ready and I downloaded Kate Mosse's walking tour, which includes snippets from "Labyrinth" at pertinent points. It's free from her website.

Our allocated room was fine enough, with a glossy and spacious bathroom. However, it had a huge glass door right in front of the bed, with only a blackout curtain. So unless one wanted to sit in the pitch dark in the middle of the day, passers-by by peered in, clearly fascinated by one's husband, spread eagled on the bed snoring while you, on hands and knees hunt in vain for a kettle, or choose your next pair of pants. You will be required to sit on the end of that bed sulking, until that husband goes off to schonk out the extra dosho to change the room for one with a bit of privacy and your own personal terrace. From that point on you will have a fabulous stay.

We wandered off downhill to the Ville Basse,

bought a sandwich and ate it on the Pont Vieux, which has the best view of La Cite in its entirety. After a mooch around the newer part of Carcassonne, with a covered market, nice squares, buzzing cafes and shops, we recrossed the bridge and began the tour, which ended a couple of hours later, not 2 minutes from the hotel. A sugar burst was required so we stopped for a cup of smoky Earl Grey and a Millefeuille at a salon de the just before the drawbridge. Afterwards we had an enjoyable sunny stroll around the whole perimeter of the city, in the gap between the inner and outer walls, called Les Lices.

After a rest and a deep, hot bubble bath (you'll need take your own lotions and potions) we went up to the bar for a Kir Royale with that stunning view of stone walls and turrets. We crossed the drawbridge again and tottered over the cobbles – not easy in a kitten heel, but I'd rather gnaw my own leg off than wear the ubiquitous trainer to go out for dinner. I'm not from Boise, Idaho.

L'Escargot is a French tapas restaurant, frequented by both locals and visitors. It was a bit too chilly to sit on the terrace, so we perched on stools inside the tiny dining room with an open kitchen, slurping Mojitos whilst staring, open-mouthed at the blackboard with its long list of tapas. It's not easy to slurp a Mojito open-mouthed and I dribbled, staining my finest Zara silk chemise. If only I'd been wearing washable lime green polyester with added Lycra.

Being both starving and indecisive, it seemed simplest just to order nearly everything. Two young chefs were waiting behind the pass in the starting position, raring to get going on the plancha. Razor clams with aioli, quail breasts with candied red pepper, escargots, roasted figs with Gorgonzola and ham, foie gras and apple compote, potatoes in BBQ sauce, skewers of juicy, pink duck, tartare of tuna with mango….. A foie gras pate de la maison came with an olive jam that was a revelation. I've got to find out how you make that. Salty. Sweet. Black and glossy. I'm all about the olive jam from here on in.

A friendly and enthusiastic young man, perhaps le patron, recommended a delicious Carcassonne wine called Vent d'Est.
It looked as though they did nice puddings, but we'd no room for a vaffer thin mint, so we just had a coffee and were brought a complimentary, sticky, orange liqueur to go with it. We thought that considering how much we'd ordered, it was incredible value and when we played "guess the bill" we were both way over. (No surprise in my case. I

always round up, unless it's shoes. But unusual for the male of the partnership.)

We preferred a lie-in to breakfast the next morning. It would have been around €15 each and probably very nice. The room had been dark and quiet, with no Nylon clad idiot dragging cases or moving the furniture at 5am as they are sometimes prone to do.

My husband had developed an unnerving fascination for dungeons, interrogation and Mediaeval punishment methods the previous day, so we were obliged to pop back over the hung, quartered and drawbridge to the Musee de l'Inquisition. It cost €9 each and after the first phase, I must confess (LOL), we were about to demand our money back. It was a series of tableaux, with soundtracks of people moaning, groaning and, unfathomably, snoring. But they'd used shop mannequins, so the effect was "Man at C&A gets his fingernails pulled out." "Man at Moss Bros points dreamily into the distance wearing this season's hessian sacking."

However, the second half was riveting and I won't spoil it for you, but man's capacity for thinking up ways of causing pain and suffering to his fellow man – and woman – is quite astounding. So I highly recommend an Autumnal minibreakholidayweekend to Carcassonne. Wandering through those ancient, empty streets in the moonlight brings the ghosts and your imagination out to play.

And not a puce fanny pack in sight.

THINGS TO DO, PLACES TO GO:

GRUISSAN – A PLAICE IN THE SUN

I recently ate two lunches in Gruissan. Not at the same time, nor even on the same day. Some might say, cruelly in my view, that they wouldn't have been surprised if I had. I may wear the odd elasticated waistband and voluminous pant item, but I am capable of restraint, even if it's not often witnessed in public. Anyway, if I was one to labour over a lettuce leaf or agonise about an aduki bean, what would there be to bore on about, as I do? As I am just about to now, in fact…….

La Perle Gruissanaise is more of a shellfish factory than a restaurant. It's right on the end of a promontory. You just keep following the road alongside the Plage des Chalets, until you drop into the sea. It's advisable to apply the brakes before that point though and there is a free car park.

"Les Chalets" that you'll pass on your way to lunch are a conurbation of raised huts, in various states of repair and style. The architectural details include sunrises, filigree, seabirds. The 19C chalets were built on stilts to counter repetitive flooding. They were rented out for beach breaks to workers before the toil of the grape harvest – a step up, literally, from covered wagons, used originally. These cabanes may have been the first French holiday park, when in the 1920's they were let out to local families and Narbonnais. They provided the atmospheric setting for the 1968 cult film "Betty Blue" about an "unbalanced and sexually aggressive free spirit".......so I picked the one I wanted, on a corner right on the beach, with dual aspect as they say on "A Place in the Sun"....but don't get me going about that again.

So back at my dream abandoned beach chalet, we were peering through the sea wind battered shutters, trying to force the locks, frolicking around on the creaking terrace "imagining ourselves with a glass of wine". My dream was snatched away later, when we discovered that they cost around a quarter of a million. Bugger me, Barry!

Moments later, at La Perle Gruissanaise, we dove upon platters of slippery oysters and plump, pink prawns. The oysters tasted of ozone, the prawns were sweet, with brown bread and butter and little jars of home made, garlicky rouille. The tables are painted Betty Blue, boats bobbed on the etang, a cold carafe of Picpoul sparkled with beads of condensation in the lunchtime sun. It's self service, you grab a bucket for discarded shells, no puddings, coffee from a vending machine. And on a gorgeous day with friends, you could have no finer feast at the Ritz. It's a lot cheaper too, at around €20 each.

The second lunch was also right next to the water, but this time it was an eerie, pale landscape, with ghostly white mounds emerging from crystalline ponds.

Salt.

La Cambuse du Saunier is the restaurant at the salt factory in Gruissan, next to a little salt museum and shop. Salt was used as currency at various times throughout history. Our word "salary" derives from it. It played a huge part in the economy and growth of this area. The museum tells some of the story and, if you'd have told me that there's only so much interest you can conjure up from salt, you'd be right! However it's worth a visit and I want some of those spiked salt shoes. They'd come in very handy for digging into the shins of anyone who spoke like an estate agent unnecessarily.

The restaurant has long trestle tables laid with individual couvert parcels wrapped in gingham cloths. The menu includes local shellfish and they specialize in cooking in a salt crust, which imparts flavour and retains the moisture of the fish or meat within.

One is brought an aperitif of Muscat whether one wants it or not, so it's a good tip to go with someone who doesn't then you can drink theirs.

For a starter we shared a tiered plat de fruits de mer. More oysters and prawns. At least I'll never get Alzheimer's. There was a study that showed that zinc helps prevent Alzheimer's and oysters are full of zinc. For a starter we shared a tiered plat de fruits de mer. More oysters and prawns. At least I'll never get Alzheimer's. There was a study that showed that zinc helps prevent Alzheimer's and oysters are full of zinc.

Most of us chose sea bass baked in a salt crust, which was succulent and fragrant. The John Dory was also good. They don't have plaice. I just needed it for the title of this piece. The accompaniment was a choice of chips, rice or legumes. I'd pictured the ubiquitous green bean, flaccid and greying, as the legume, but actually it was a rather chic looking glass bowlful of ratatouille.

There was bread, cold white wine and efficient, if robotic service. I think the thing is that they have quite a few coach parties, come, quite rightly, to gaze at the lunar landscape and the vicious salt shoes. So the

service is functional rather than personal.
However it was a very well cooked lunch, in
an incredible setting. They've recently
opened up a cocktail bar, which would be a
beautiful place to come for a saline rimmed
sundowner. Lunch cost approximately €35
per head, with ice cream and coffee. Well
worth its salt.
It would be advisable to book, given the
coach party issue and also.........it's seasonal!
Ohhhh.....I kill myself sometimes!

So shake it on over to Gruissan, gorge
yourself on zinc and a variety of salt based
products. Have a dip in the briny, fantasise
about your own beachside pied a terre and
then go home and hurl cake at the
television. It's the perfect day.

THINGS TO DO, PLACES TO GO:

LAC DE JOUARRES - MEXICANS AND WAVES

The setting of La Guinguette du Lac is beautiful, right on the lake. In the daytime you can watch windsurfers madly whipping up a froth and clinging on for dear life – being hurled thought the air while trying to grasp a wet pole and balance on an ironing board. In the evening, equally thrilling in its way, you can gaze out at the sun dipping into the water like the maraschino cherry in your Vermouth.

You can swim, throw yourself off the raft, hire a kayak, picnic – all under the watchful eye of the lifeguards. You can park your car and it's all free. The French are so good at lakes.

The eating area of the café is half in, half out, so if the wind is too much – and it can get breezy – ask those windsurfers – you can sit at a huge window inside.

The atmosphere is casual, with many of the clients coming from the nearby holiday houses and campervans. But there are also regulars, families, groups of locals. The

patron is always friendly and welcoming.
On this particular evening, we had one tuna
tartare and one dish of snails to start with.
The snails were, I'm reliably informed, good
ones. I am a game gal and will try anything
– ask those windsurfers – but I do balk at
snails due to an unfortunate encounter with
an enormous slug, which traumatised me for
life. If anyone can enlighten me about just
what the point of slugs is, I'd be interested
to hear it.

But, back at the escargots, I can personally
attest to the fact that a bit of crusty
baguette dipped into their garlicky, parsley
butter, was mouthwatering. The tuna, fresh
and with lashings of lemon juice, was
reminiscent of a great ceviche I once had in
Acapulco. This was a spooky coincidence
because there happened to be live music at
La Guinguette and the band was called
"Mexican Blues". As it turned out were about
as Mexican as a tin of supermarket Chilli Con
Carne, but it didn't matter as they were
excellent musicians and the volume was just
right, so as not to quash conversation.

The entrecôte was well cooked and
flavoursome, with crunchy chips and a
strong Roquefort sauce. My husband's Duck
Burger with Foie Gras (ooooohhhh get HIM,
being all adventurous tonight) was delicious
and the burger was drenched with unctuous

juice from the generous portion of foie gras
sitting on top.
We'd had aperitifs, two demis of red wine
and the bill was around €80. We cycled back
over the vineyards, just a little wobblier than
on the outward journey, with full tummies
and smiles on our faces, humming "Girl from
Ipanema".

This is a good place to take visitors and
guests because of the view and, the fact that
you can just have drinks / coffee / ice
cream, or one or two courses if you feel like
it. And you can swim before or afterwards.
There are nice salads for a light lunch. Live
music on Sunday nights through the
Summer and wonderful sunsets.

RIBA RIBA.

THINGS TO DO, PLACES TO GO:

LEUCATE PLAGE – BEACH FOAM

The thing about the seaside is, that no matter what the weather, there's always some brave sod valiantly trying to enjoy themselves. We picked the only cold, cloudy, drizzly day since records began – well, in two months anyway – to book a sleepover at the beach.

Nevertheless, people were having raucous al fresco lunches wearing waterproofs over their best linen, walking on the rain pitted sand and playing beach games with wind-wayward balls.
So we joined in.

We checked in to our hotel, La Cote Revee, on Leucate Plage. Our room, around €78 for the night, was bright, clean and cheerful, with a balcony looking straight on to the beach. Nothing fancy: no Bulgari products, Egyptian cotton robes or iPod docks here, but everyone was friendly and helpful and we had everything we needed.
We walked down the beach for about half an hour to the Oyster Village. Boats pull up at the back of the little restaurants and heap their bounty directly on to your plats de fruits de mer. We had a plate of oysters,

mussels and amazingly tasty crevettes, brown bread and butter and a bottle of Picpoul de Pinet. The bill was around €23. I couldn't tell you which restaurant it was, apart from that it had orange plastic chairs, but I'm sure it wouldn't really matter as the seafood is fresh and the prices similar in all of them.

After a windswept meander back along the surf, foam sizzling around our flip flops, there was nothing for it but to have a delicious snooze in the room. We had a little wander in the rain and a cup of tea with a soggy newspaper, then headed back for hot showers and a bit of lippie. My husband didn't do the lippie thing. Though given half a chance……..I digress.

Another stroll down la plage to our dinner destination, Chez Biquet, which resembles a large wooden beach shack. There are driftwood sculptures on the sand, alongside chairs and curtained cubicles. Sadly empty on this windswept evening, I'd imagine they would be packed full when there's a balmy sunset to sip cocktails by.

We perched at the bar and ordered Margaritas! Well, so what if it was cold. The decor is industrial and eclectic. Tolyx tables, huge rusting factory lamps, mid century plastic moulded chairs, bleached driftwood partitions. The staff were young and cool.Vintage silent movies were playing on a big screen. Laid back lobsters blew bubbles inthe tank. We couldn't decide on two starters, so weordered three. Blame the weathe1: Sardinesand onions served in the tin, with crispy croutons and chorizo butte2: Oysters. You can never have too many ina day.3: A pot of steaming mussels in a ginger broth.

One of the main courses was the thickest, freshest, rarest tuna we've eaten this side of Tokyo. The other, was sole in a creamy foam with carrot purée and roasted peppers. I have been a bit scathing about the concept of foam in the past. A bit of a foam party pooper. But here, it seemed quite appropriate and very delicious I have to admit.Chocolate fondants with salted caramel ice cream for pudding. Bill: €120 We ordered a bio wine and won't bother again, but a final glass of Chardonnay left a nicer taste before the starlit stroll back to our beachside bed.

The next morning we were nervous about opening the shutters and it seemed awfully quiet out there…..but…..

" Wait a minute, it stopped raining.
Guys are swimming, gals are sailing.
Playing beach ball, gee that's betta,
Muddah, Fadduh,kindly disregard this letter!"

THINGS TO DO, PLACES TO GO:

VALRAS PLAGE – MAD RAG & WILD TURBOT

Despite the fact that Valras Plage is a relatively short distance from home, we fancied a minibreak rather than a day trip, in order to enjoy long, unhurried hours on the beach and a slap up seafood dinner. The journey, however, was somewhat stressful due to the enthusiasm of one driver of a huge red lorry, to join us in the back seat of our little Renault.

I don't know if it was our UK plates, our jaunty cabriolet or an urge to discuss the wider implications of Brexit, but he was honking his horn and waving. Such was the level of his desperation to make our acquaintance, he drove so close up our rear end, not only could we see the whites of his eyes, but the blood vessels pulsing in his face and the baring of his teeth.

Sadly, we eventually had to turn off the big main road, otherwise I think he probably would have literally pushed us all the way to Montpelier. Lorry drivers are so helpful aren't they? I bet he collects for charity, or works with children and animals in his spare time, perhaps at a Rottweiler rescue centre.

The Albizzia hotel was therefore a welcome sight as we chose a space in their car park and limped, pale and trembling into the shady, fragrant foyer. The welcome from M. le Patron and his wife was extremely friendly – the peaceful ambiance, instantly relaxing.

Our room was a triple, the last one left. One double and one single bed. I suppose that would have been excellent news for some couples, married for a considerable number of years now, devoted to one another but getting on one another's wick, personal space wise. I don't know, I'm just saying…….*

The room was decorated in cool whites and greys, nothing fancy – simple but clean and comfortable. There was a nice bathroom with generous, soft towels and products – we like a product (particularly one delicious orange and cinnamon shower gel). There was a separate loo. Also excellent news. See above. *

We had a balcony with table and chairs, overlooking the pool, the sea was visible a couple of blocks away. There was a TV and good, free wifi which was even available all around the swimming pool.

We headed straight down there via the bar and ordered a Coke and a beer, resisting the urge for two large brandies, PTTD – Post Traumatic Truck Disorder. They insisted on bringing the drinks out to us, which typified the quality of service throughout our short stay.
(No lunch or dinner is served.)

The pool was surrounded by sun beds upon which couples read, snoozed and chatted in hushed tones. Mostly French, there was only one other English set. I suspect they may have been of German descent though, call me old fashioned, it was just a funny little intuitive feeling. I must have noticed a slight inflection in their accent, or turn of a

Teutonic jawline as I passed them on the same sun beds…..all day long…… from the break of dawn til dusk…… their towels acting as striped guardians if they were ever momentarily absent.
Anyway, after a couple of blissful hours here, we strolled the 5 minutes to the beach where we found Oasis. NO silly, not the Gallagher's, reunited and strumming in the sand, but a beach bar where we had a lovely plate of tapas and a carafe of rose.

We swam in the briny, read for a while, got sandblasted and sunburnt so eventually beat a retreat back to the peaceful haven of the Albizzia pool, where a tray of tea and biscuits was delivered to our loungers – the ones just next to the English-of-German-descent couple, who were being turned for bed sores.

We agreed at that point, that if we'd paid ten times our rate (€115 including tax) we really could not have been having a better time, except that there'd be someone coming round to clean our sunglasses, which gets on your nerves anyway.

After a lovely hot shower with some of that gorgeous orangey stuff, we wandered down the beach for fifteen minutes to the center of town, in search of cocktails. My husband almost made a run for it, when heading towards us came two outrageously decorated Caiprihnas. Big plastic flowers and sundry items hanging off the edge of the oversized coupes. Sophisticated moi! It was just like one of Delboy's cocktails off "Only Fools and Horses". The world was our lobster.

Our hotelier had recommended his favourite restaurant – La Madrague.

La Madrague is slightly off the beaten track, but it's worth the extra few minutes stroll along the harbour from the epicenter of Valras Plage. This also means that it has less the feel of a brash holiday/tourist restaurant and more that of a rather classy local's institution. Less a bum bag, sock and sandal – more a linen trouser and a kitten heel.

The interior is cool and airy – ceiling fans, bleached wood, neutrals and whites. No fishing nets and glass balls stapled to the ceiling here. Not an orange wall, plastic mermaid or fluorescent bulb in sight. Yay! We hadn't booked (and we were, in fact, tourists) so were placed on the outer edge of the room. We had a good view of the goings on and the port though. Next time we'll reserve a table on the terrace or in the swing of things.

We ordered coupes of champagne to begin

proceedings and relished in rolling the bubbles over our tongues whilst reading the menu. Gazing at the boats rocking in the harbour. A balmy sea breeze ruffling the pristine tablecloths. The happy chatter, clanks and smells of a busy but smoothly run operation. It imbued confidence in a good night ahead. Apart from finding a tenner on the pavement, what finer feeling?

We had one order of oysters, fresh and beautifully presented on a mound of ice and seaweed. We also started with the plumpest razor clams we've had, juicy and swimming in persillade, that required chunks of baguette dipped in and then wiped around the plate. Never mind decorum when there's parsley flavoured butter to be mopped up.

Our main courses were one special of turbot sauvage and another of scallops with chorizo. The wild turbot was huge, creamy – sliding off the bone and swimming silkily into the bouche. The scallops were equally succulent and that garlicky, smoky, spicy chorizo combo works so well. Whoever thought of that in the first place anyway? Was it the same person that thought up Bayonne ham with figs? Or M&Ms with salted popcorn? Or Jaffa Cakes with Stilton……or is that just me.
Each main course came with three little ramekins, filled with delicious vegetables:

ratatouille; creamed spinach; mashed potato with rouille.

We had a bottle of Languedoc white wine, from an extensive and, I'm assured by those who care about that stuff, reasonably priced list.

Tragically, we were too full for anything else and wanted to wander off around town for a coffee, so we stopped there. The bill was around €90.

Call me paranoid, but in the very first instance, I felt that perhaps our welcome wasn't as unconditionally warm as it might have been because we were the dreaded bemused and wide eyed tourist, about to murder the menu with ghastly pronunciation and hunting down well done steak. However, the service was excellent and everyone was very friendly and chatty once we'd explained that our hotel manager had recommended the restaurant as one of his own personal favourites. Either way, we can't wait to go back whether they want us there or not. Bonus fact: La Madrague is not a jittery J-Cloth, it's a large sort of fishing net used to catch tuna. Don't say I never learn you nuffing.

After dinner we called in at the little fairground near the hotel, played a few games, had a scream down the giant slide and raced virtual motorbikes. As I said……sophisticated.

We had a great night's sleep with no noise at all. Not even some idiot doing Riverdance in the room above or dragging suitcases at 5.00am, as some hotel lunatics are driven to do.

Hang on though……lunatics……driven……it would soon be time to hit the road. But not before a fresh and tasty breakfast (croissants, yogurt, eggs, juice, cereal) and another hour or two by that tranquil pool. And yes, they WERE still there.

THINGS TO DO, PLACES TO GO:

AVIGNON & ORANGE – GET AWAY

Money. Get away. What can you do with one euro today?

Well, you could go to Avigon, in Provence, by train.
OK – you may need to get a degree in Logistics and then an MSc in Computer Sciences to work out how to buy the ticket on-line, but once you have, the Languedoc is your huitre. So pack a picnic (local trains.....no buffet car.....I can testify......staggered up and down clutching coffee money in sweaty fist for half an hour before I twigged........maintained cool.....don't think anyone noticed) and enjoy the scenery. No traffic, manic motorway or parking stress. You are delivered into the center of your chosen city.

And it's ONE EURO.

So one shiny Summer's day, we caught a mid morning train from the glorious station at Narbonne, which reeks Allo Allo with every brass door handle and gauze curtain. The train hugs the coastline all the way so etangs, flamingoes, surf and wild marshes flash by as you flick through your mag, nibbling on your Salade Nicoise from the station buffet. We arrived in Avignon exactly on time and our hotel, Cloitre Saint Louis, was 5 minutes walk from the station. It's virtually opposite the tourist office, packed with bewildered, bridge-hunting masses, causing sparks, as they bump aimlessly into one another, clad in tracksuits of static laden man-made fabrics, in Any Colour You Like.

Once inside the stone arch of the hotel, away from the dust and sirens of the main thoroughfare, we were swallowed up by a calm, shady 15C cloister with a huge burbling, moss cloaked fountain tinkling in the middle. Breathe. Our room was in the old part of the hotel. It had low windows that looked out onto time worn walls and terracotta roof tiles. It was subtly decorated and contemporary, with a nice bathroom containing actual products, rather than the increasingly common, giant squeezy bottle of washing up liquid nailed to the wall. This sends an immediate message of both meanness and mistrust. And anyway, if you've flown, they are over the 100ml hand luggage allowance. Though it's handy to carry a screwdriver if your checking a bag, in which case they do remove quite easily.

Anyway, back in the room, we also had genuine Mediaeval free Wi-Fi, tea and coffee making facilities and a very helpful chap called Kevin in Reception. There was a restaurant and cozy bar. It cost around €140. We went out to explore and became absorbed in the back streets of Avignon. We are probably the only people in the world to have bothered neither with the Pont nor the Palais des Popes. Instead we found Rue des Teinturiers ~ Street of the Dyers – so called because in the 15th century, it was the hub of wool and silk manufacture, as well as dyeing, in the town. In the 17th and 18th centuries, those typically Provencal patterned textiles, Indian inspired – "les indiennes" – were produced here, when they'd been banned in other parts of France.

This tiny cobbled street has a fascinating history and runs alongside the River Sorgue, punctuated by watermills, which fed the textile and dyeing workshops. Now there are numerous cafes, bars, vintage and quirky, independent shops selling design and crafts, fashion and furniture. That Fat Old Sun started to throb, so we headed back to Cloitre Saint Louis make full use of our facilities, specifically the rooftop pool. A swimming pool, a sunbed, an iPod, a chilled glass of Picpoul. We wrote some postcards. "Wish you were here."

Because I'm good at this stuff, I'd researched an out of the way dinner destination in advance. The thing is that Avignon is all about that bridge and that

Palais de Popes. So avoid them.

Back in Rue des Teinturiers, "L'Offset" is a sublime combination of typography and food. If you happen to be a Graphic Designer, like wot moi is, you'll adore it. If your not, you'll love it anyway. An old print shop, with original presses and ephemera, in an industrial building turned restaurant.

We sat at the bar with a couple of Caiprihnas – cold, sour, salty, sugary and strong. We ate on the cobbled terrace out front, the watermills splish sploshing away. Their formule for €22 offered us Clafoutis aux girolles, Duo de Foie Gras, mi-cuit en terrine et poêlé sur pain perdu, Duck in a honey sauce and a Chocolat Melty in the Middle, with something salted and caramel on the side. Very good value and very good cooking. A Helvetica of a meal.

Our whole reason for taking this trip was because my husband had procured some tickets for a concert at the Roman amphitheatre in Orange. This had taken him hours of subversive correspondence with complete strangers and highly exciting bidding action. After a bargain lunch of Carpaccio amid the market traders and a bit of shopping in Les Halles we caught the train out to Orange. Ze man in ze black jacket under ze sign of ze museum handed over the tickets, offered us various pharmaceutical products hidden in his sock (which we obviously refused – I mean, we ARE from Surrey) and disappeared into the night. We found our cold, stone seats, upon which many a Roman buttock had clenched. Others, more savvy, had brought cushions. We however, ended up with bums Comfortably Numb. We watched David Gilmour (him off Pink Floyd) deliver a gob smacking, tear inducing performance with lights, smoke and audience wailing along, in a magical setting.

The thing is about The Dave is, he's dead posh. When he thanked the band it was like a headmaster making his address at a parent's evening. "I'd like to thank my team for their sterling efforts tonight. Would you kindly allow me to introduce my drummer." Sadly we had to rely on M. Le Pharmacie dans les Feet for a lift back to Avignon. While I tried to make conversation with his Hungarian girlfriend, crammed in the back of his tiny car, my husband valiantly attempted to remind him of the speed limits and offer helpful safety tips for keeping a car attached to the tarmac on all four of its wheels. On approaching Avignon I noticed we were heading for a huge, illuminated bridge. Blimey, I thought, he's not going over that is he? Only half of it's been finished! Only when we were back, trembling and thankful, was I finally let in on the full extent of our chauffeur's Brain Damage. But he was a bloody nice bloke. I think we've arranged to meet him for a drink in London. Gawd help us.

Avignon is a splendid destination. We must all use the marvelous €1 train service anyway, in case they change their minds and take it away. We're in the hi-fidelity first class traveling set. Who needs a Lear Jet?

THINGS TO DO, PLACES TO GO: ARLES - ARLES BE SEEING YOU

Picasso and Perfume on a Provençal minibreak.
After a painless – nay and thrice nay – enjoyable train ride from Narbonne to Arles, one glorious September morning, the husband rattled our case over cobbles, past the ancient Roman amphitheatre towards the Hotel du Forum.

Following a heated debate over our exact whereabouts (some people, not me, don't deserve an iPhone if they can't even work the navigation) we stumbled upon the Place du Forum and were smacked straight in the eye by the garish yellow awning of Cafe de la Nuit. This is where Van Gogh sat on his actual oil stained bottom and quaffed absinthe until his ear dropped off The square is packed with cafes and bars, terraces and tables – waiters hurling themselves through gaps laden with coffees, plates of paella and colourful cocktails. Yes, it's touristy, of course. But there was a festive atmosphere and one bar that was to become our regular, served a Fig Margarita for €5 a shot.

The hotel was in the hub of things and had a more impressive entrance than our Booking.Com rate would suggest – shiny Belle Époque tiles, engraved glass and polished brass. We checked in; we found our room; I sulked about the view; we asked to change rooms; he paid the extra – as is all customary on any minibreak. This room was huge, nothing fancy but clean, with good beds and a wonderful view of tiled rooftops with the shady oasis of a pool below. Having spent months in small villages, albeit peaceful and pretty, a bustling town with chic shops where you can buy things – you know, actual real things other than a baguette – was a bit of a treat. Apart from marvellous souvenir emporiums draped with Starry Night T-towels, fridge magnets and mouse mats, there were boutiques, galleries, papetieres and parfumeries. One proffered a perfume called "Arlesienne" which evoked rose gardens, Provençal saffron and Fig Margaritas. Hints dropped and splattered on the Roman cobblestones like coins in a fountain.

On the first Wednesday of every month there is a brocante/vide grenier along the tree lined Boulevard des Lices. This was one such day!

There were mountains of white, embroidered linens; silverware; Art Deco statuettes; 1950's posters; coins; vintage cameras and glass. There were bird tables; spanners; postcards; lanterns; books and badges. We bought a sommelier's wine tasting dish and a zinc-kitchen-tool-holder-thing. You can also find the tourist office here, as well as Bar du Marche, an atmospheric local's bar, with the aroma of Pastis and pétanque on the television.

After tea and cake – so many bars, cafes, salons de the to choose from – we had a cool swim and a hot shower (take your own luxurious toiletry produits). Then it just had to be done – an apero at the Van Gogh cafe. It was an expensive tourist trap but the waiter, a contemporary of Vincent's by the look of him, was charming. Take a peek inside too, at the evocative zinc bar and velvet drapery.

The notion of the Baby Bistro is a blinder. You get to sample a Michelin chef's food at a fraction of the price and, without all that whispering and people in dark suits sneaking up on you like Ninjas to refold your napkin. And who needs a load of cloches lifted at exactly the same time anyway. You could get concussion.

We've tried a few in Paris and they were excellent, so when I read about Jean-Luc Rabanel's Baby Bistro "A Côté" in Arles, it was a natural selection. M. Rabanel is the master of organic vegetables, or as he puts it, "Greenstronomy". Normally I hold no truc with such overpriced, overhyped nonsense but when the chef has 2 Michelin stars, owning the first organically-certified restaurant to be awarded that honour, I'll put my prejudices a cote.

Down a tiny pedestrian street in Arles, casual yet smart – yes, let's say shmasual – tables nestle on the terrace of the shiny, big-Daddy-posh-restaurant. Inside there, shady figures tugged at their cuffs and hoisted enormous cloches simultaneously, innocent diners knocked unconscious in their wake, reviving only to swoon once again at the sight of their bill. Meanwhile, outside, you can relax and sip a cold coupe, while perusing your choices from a 32€ menu de marche.

Call me old fashioned, but I think an entree of oysters and foie gras proposes two of the finest things you can put in your mouth at the same time. With dainty garnishes of Camargue salt and sweet onion confit, the foie gras melted on the tongue and the oysters, spiked with shallot vinegar, washed down the throat like tingling surf. Himself chose a sticky lamb confit for the main course with, as you'd expect, exquisite vegetables. But we were at the gateway to the Camargue, with its bulls, white horses and cowboys – or guardians. So I had to have Guardian de Taureau Tartare, the raw version of the indigenous stew. It was so fresh and soft, my closest analogy was a sashimi of fatty tuna consumed in the fish market in Tokyo. On top of this juicy mound – studded with olives, peppers and tomatoes – was a wobbling egg yolk which coated the meat with an ochre emulsion when speared. My matador and I shared cheese supplied by Bernard Rattalinond, Fromager and luscious lemon tart, which started off all sophisticated and romantic enough, until we tasted it and forks were drawn like picas in a bullring. I would only caution you not to accept the table beside the window, next to the digital screen displaying a slideshow of the cuisine. It's a cause of fascination to every passer by, who stops and stares at it – and therefore unavoidably at you – while you slobber oysters, drip runny egg down your chin and fight unceremoniously over a pudding.

Apart from that I recommend "A Côté" and will never sneer at an overpriced organic turnip in Sainsbury's again.

PS: I'm sure a meal in the main restaurant is splendid. I have no actual grounds for accusing them of attacking diners with serving dishes. But it has a great reputation so one day I might just grab it by the horns.

It befell us to try a couple of nightcaps in the fun-filled Place, where we joined in with some open air dancing action spilling out from a bar with a DJ and a gypsy band. The Gypsy Kings are from here and Spanish guitar music is all around.

The next morning brought searing heat; a crowded bus terminal; an excursion into the Camargue and a banging hangover. But I rallied for your sakes and in the interest of research, bravely enjoyed a fabulous day out which culminated in Caiprihnas back at our hotel pool bar. Then some delicious tapas in an old, dark bistro favoured by Matadors, strewn with posters of bullfights and courses camarguaises.

 In the morning there was time, before the train home, to immerse myself in Picasso drawings and Christian Lacroix (born in Arles) designs at the Musee Reassu, cloistered and crouching over the Rhone. Arles has history, art, food, shopping, music, cocktails and romance. We were smitten. I have to admit to a bit of a moistening of the eye as the train lurched away. When a pink, cellophane wrapped box of L'Occitane "Arlesienne" was whipped out and placed in front of me, it turned to full on slobbering sobs.

As romantic mementos go, this was better than an ear any day.

THINGS TO DO, PLACES TO GO

THE CAMARGUE

"On white horses let me ride away

To my world of dreams so far away

Let me run

To the sun...."

Thursday tea times after school, the highlight of the week. A tinned salmon sandwich and "The White Horses" on telly. Since then, one of my many, many obsessions has been to visit the Camargue. I've no idea why, because that programme was set in Eastern Europe. And it was about the Lipizzaners. But Geography never was my strong point, so the Camargue it had to be.

We caught a bus from the terminal in Arles, which perked up the male traveller no end, because it cost a paltry €1 for the 45 minute trip. After an interesting mini tour of the outskirts of Arles, the countryside spread away on either side, as flat as a green tie-dyed tablecloth, strewn with the brown and white crumbs of scrub and egrets.

We rolled past ranches, pampas grass, marshes, reeds and ponds hitching up at the last staging post, the seaside village of Sainte Mairie de la Mer. We ate huge tuna baguettes and gulped ice cold Coke at a shaded sandwich bar near the bus stop, planning our afternoon. (We also got to choose a cake for the bus ride home. All part of a €4 "Meal Deal" which even tops Gregg's. Apart, of course, from their sausage rolls which can't be beaten.)

There was a boat trip later, giving us time to
buy pouches of salt and bottles of cowboy
rice beer, fill a plastic water bottle with
Camargue Muscat, wander paella lined
streets and have a cool swim in the denim
blue sea. The cruise was €4.50 per person.
We slid into seats on the top deck and ate
our cakes. Geography AND willpower…..not
my strong points. We enjoyed a two hour
cruise up the Petit Rhone and into deepest
cowboy country. We spied small, waterside
wooden chalets beside which big, square
nets were slung from trees and poles, poised
to drop straight down into the river.

As the cabins disappeared, marshes and rice
paddies emerged, coming alive with wading
birds, black bulls and yes, the white
horses……

"Where the clouds are made of candy floss
As the day is born
When the stars are gone
We'll race to meet the dawn…."

The boat pulled up at a grassy bank and
there was a cloud of dust in the distance. As
it got nearer, we heard the thud of hooves
on dry mud. From the brown mist a herd of
bulls and horses emerged driven on by a
guardian. It was staged but, call me easily
pleased, strangely thrilling. The rest of the
cruise took in further stunning scenery and

more beasts. Clusters of horses and their brown young sipped the salty water. They are, unusually, born brown and turn grey as they grow older. They are the oldest living breed of horse, with friendly, curious temperaments. I wanted to take some home.

(We were on holiday in Tunisia once and we were offered 40 camels for our daughter. Well, we'd never have got them on the plane. Similar problem here I'm afraid, only with a Renault Megane and a cross channel ferry.)

"Where the clouds are made of candy floss
As the day is born
When the stars are gone
We'll race to meet the dawn.........oh, alright, I'll shut up now. I'm even getting on my own nerves and that's saying something.

When it was time to turn the boat around, the captain put his foot down. We skidded and skipped across the waves that batter each other as the Rhone collides with the Mediterranean. It was a bit of a bonus white knuckle ride, complete with splash zone. Good job I'd had the foresight to eat that cake! Geography, willpower, humility........I was almost hoping that we'd miss our bus back as there was a tiny oyster shack in the port, doing a special huitre/vin blanc apero deal for €7. You could have a good night out in Sainte Mairie de la Mer.

There are plenty of restaurants, bars and a jolly seaside atmosphere, sprinkled with a seasoning of Camargue spice. There's also the bull ring, the church, the tower, the gypsy festival, the statue of Black Sarah, the ornithological park, the ranches, the flamingoes, the riding and the mosies on through the wilderness.

So, we'll be galloping back there when we can for a proper stay, but as an easy, affordable and fun day trip from Arles it hits the bullseye. Yeeehaa!

THINGS TO DO, PLACES TO GO

ON THE ROAD

By now you may be anticipating Summer
visitations from those beloved and sadly
missed friends and family back in the
Motherland. Those few special people (the
cast of Ben Hur) who pop in (stay too long)
and respect your lovely French home (treat
it like a B&B) full of appreciation and
gratitude (drink all your wine).
Anyway, here are a few suggestions of
reasonably priced places for them to stop off
at on the drive down here, in order to
enhance their trip (delay their arrival time).
They are all to be found en route to the
Languedoc from the UK, and are highly
recommended as a night's stay, for those
special people in your lives (never liked them
anyway).

Hotel du Tribunal
4, Place du Palais, 61400 Mortagne-au-Perche, Haut Normandie

After a long day of ferries and driving, we
arrived at Le Tribunal at about 8.15pm.
Consequently, we were tired and stressed,
but nevertheless really excited about it. We
knew what to expect – the leafy little square,
the cozy, chic foyer, the comfortable room –

and what we were looking forward to most, what we had come back a second time for – the delicious dinner. Our room was bright and fresh, looking out on to a courtyard. We freshened up and went down for an aperitif. A jolly lady came and brought delicious nibbles and the menus. Dinner was again amazing. A pate de foie gras with pistachios accompanied by a little shot of foie gras milkshake with a froth of almond cream. A plate of tomatoes – but like no other, green ones treated in such a way as to make them soft and concentrated, a gazpacho "terrine", a tomato sorbet. Then black pudding tasting like a mouthful of Xmas, guinea fowl with a sticky, tangy sweet orange sauce, cinnamon and caramel rice pudding and wonderful cheese. It was the best meal we'd had in a long time. And it was €30 each. We slept well, had an early coffee, ready to hit the road feeling refreshed and ready to face the dreaded peage once again. A piece of advice though. If you expect to arrive after 6.00pm, phone ahead to warn them and confirm your dinner reservation. Le Tribunal is a special place, in a pretty town. A favourable verdict

Auberge les Glycines
Avenue des Pyrenees, 47290 Cancon

Our room was basic but fine. After a stressful day on the Autoroute, I was looking forward to a hot bath but there was no plug.

Great efforts were made by the staff to find one, which they did.

We had a snooze, then a cup of tea by the pool. It was a shame that it was unseasonably chilly, so we didn't feel like going for a dip. However it was extremely pleasant to sit around with a drink, and we could have been in a chi chi boutique hotel – nice loungers surrounded by lush vegetation.

We came down to dinner refreshed and in a cloud of nice smelling products (our own. Remember to take yours). We had a glass of Floc for an aperitif and sat down to dinner in a tastefully decorated dining room. It would be lovely to sit outside to eat on a balmy evening. Dinner was delicious – foie gras, smoked duck, confit – regional produce which was well cooked and carefully presented.

After a digestif on the terrace we tottered up to bed. Unfortunately, there was a young family nearby with a screaming baby. We've all been there and I know it's hard, but after an hour we had to ring reception with the idea that we might move rooms as it was impossible to sleep. The manager could hear the disturbance through the phone and instantly ran up the stairs, knocked on the family's door and, I don't know how or why, but the problem just went away. We were

VERY impressed and proceeded to get a good night's sleep. He could have just given the ubiquitous shrug and let us get on with it! I would highly recommend both the hotel and restaurant for a stopover.

Citotel Les Alizes, (at Bellegarde Airport) Limoges, Haute Vienne, Limousin

After a few hot, sweaty hours on the road, this hotel provided a cheapish, basic but cool and quiet stopover. It was €70 a night for a double room overlooking flowerbeds. There was no bath, but a shower, TV and clean sheets. The bonus is the pool which was quiet and refreshing, with only the drone of the occasional light aircraft drifting up into the early evening skies. We spent a nice couple of hours here, with tea and later a kir & a beer, before showering for a lovely dinner at the airport restaurant a few steps away. You can sit on the terrace and watch the little planes coming and going as you eat. Breakfast was an extra €7 pp – juice, hot drinks, yogurts, cheese, croissants & jam. The room was quiet during the night, but hot and stuffy, so noisier with the window open as lorries trailed past

Hotel la Truite Dore
Rue de la Barre, 46090 Vers, Cahors, France

This hotel is in a pretty Lot village, right on the river with the clank of boules and the rushing of water on stone. The staff are welcoming and helpful. On arrival you can have a swim in the pool, or a drink on your own little terrace if your are in the right room. We saw most of them, given that my husband had a bad knee and we had to have a scenic tour of the whole range of accommodation on offer before he found one that suited. Even then, the staff were still friendly. Still helpful. We booked the Demi-Pension because it was a bargain and had a very delicious dinner on a lovely terrace. I'd actually go back and stay a bit longer at this one, as the hotel is great and the area looks really interesting

THINGS TO DO, PLACES TO GO

I LOVE PARIS….

"I love Paris in the spring time
I love Paris in the fall
I love Paris in the winter when it drizzles
I love Paris in the summer when it sizzles"

Cole Porter

Pink blooms of the first bare arms and legs.
Cherry blossoms tremor as the warm breeze
ruffles virginal leaves and the hems of
flowery skirts in Les Tuileries.
Summer: sizzling on a deck chair along the
sanded banks of the Seine. Watching open
air movies with a picnic. Popping corks and
topping up at the pop up champagne bar
atop the Eiffel Tower.
Autumn: the toasty/sweet scent of scolding
chestnuts and wading through crunchy,
copper leaves in the Luxembourg Gardens.

But now it's Winter and the rain slick, black
streets are glossy with the reflected lights of
taxis. Your fingers are cold and puckered by
sodden gloves. It's lunchtime, so duck into
La Cremerie du Polidor in the 6th
Arrondissement. You're swallowed up by
warmth and the smell of onions, roasted
meats and steamed potatoes. Dishes of

escargots, kidneys in mustard, guinea fowl with cabbage and boeuf bourgignon whizz by. A plate is smashed and there's a deafening chorus of "Bravo". A waiter argues loudly with a customer over a tip. It's full of Parisians on their lunch break, shoppers with huge Printemps bags, tourists cowering from the waiters. They are frozen and soaked, having been trudging the streets since their crack-of-dawn croissants. Their shell suits are glistening with rain drops.

There are elderly gentlemen who come every day and sit in the same place, as did Hemmingway and Kerouac. Through the back are old wooden drawers where they used to keep their own personal napkins.

If no queue, you are squeezed in along an endless communal table. Order a couple of Cremants de Bourgogne and chat to your elbow to elbow neighbours about the weather. The bubbles and the warmth begin to permeate. Another plate is smashed somewhere.

Order cold pike pate, egg mayonnaise and a carafe of house red to go with your roast chicken and mash. The lemon pie is legendary. It would be churlish to go back out into the rain without a thimbleful of dark coffee and a sticky Cointreau. Everybody

else is and no one's in a hurry to leave. Even
the tourists are a little less wide eyed and
trembling as they dig around in their kagouls
for an extra euro's tip beneath the stare of
the waiter.

Round the corner is a chic little hotel, Villa
Madame, full of scented candles and
antiques. The rooms are small but
comfortable. Tiny dark green bottles of
Hermes Orange Blossom products nestle
amongst fluffy white towels. There's a small
bar and a courtyard where you can sip a G&T
swathed in their cashmere blankets. You –
not the G&T. Well, the ice would melt. If
you'd prefer to look down on the city from
on high, tottering up and down vertiginous,
slippery stone steps whilst clinging on to an
iron handrail for dear life, god (pick
whichever one you like) invented
Montmartre. Stay at Hotel La Terrasse,
where you can go to sleep with the Eiffel
Tower twinking "Bonne Nuit" at you over the
rooftops.

In the morning tousle with tassels, feel fabric
and barter for buttons in the haberdashery
district at the foot of La Butte. Your husband
may glaze over and wander off. Who
wouldn't find joy in metres of Toile de Jouy?
But you can find him gazing up at Picasso's
old studio, or down at Montmartre's very
own working vineyard.

Book supper at La Balancoire, a local's bistro – a huge blackboard, forks that float magically above the tables and a real swing. The food is good too.

We're off again to another neighbourhood, just to the right….or left…..depending on which way you're facing. Geography never was my strong point. I research the hotels and restaurants and Passepartout gets us there. Luckily, usually they're in the same city, thought there WAS that time in Rome……….What's a €50 taxi fare in the grand scheme of things anyway? I don't know what all the fuss was about.

Anyway, my unerring compass of fun is now pointing at Canal St Martin, in the 10th, within walking distance of Gare du Nord. If you're not wearing kitten heels. The canal banks are lined with design and architectural book shops, independent fashion retailers, bars and cafes. One of best shops in the world resides here, Antoine at Lilli, choc full of multicoloured crockery, cutlery, candles, Indian mirrors, lamps, fairy lights, Mexican oilcloth, trays, bells and whistles. Great for Xmas decorations.

You could have a coffee or cocktail at Chez Prune, but you'd better be wearing black, or else something that looks like you bought it from a vide grenier, but actually cost more than your first car. You could swig Malbec and munch on charcuterie at the best wine bar of all, the diminutive Verre Vole. OR go for a fragrant, spicy, cheap Cambodian lunch at the friendly Petit Cambodge, before leaping aboard a boat ride that goes underneath, yes underneath the Bastille and into central Paris.

You may have lingered in the Louvre and been overwhelmed by the crowds and queues, so pop next door to its less famous neighbour, La Musee des Arts Decoratifs. They have toys, advertising and graphics as well as absolutely fabulous fashion exhibitions, from Jackie Onassis's wardrobe, to Vionnet's artful drapes and Miyake's pristine pleats. There's also a garden and cafe with one of the best views of La Tour. Have a stroll through the adjoining Tuileries, along whose grey, gravelled paths an impoverished Hemmingway used to push an old pram in which to secrete the pigeons he'd just nobbled for his supper. You could take a ride on the festive Ferris wheel and watch the Xmas lights trickling down the Champs Elysees. Just across Rue Rivoli, is Angelina, an elegant, marbled salon du the. Ladies sip Lapsang and nibble on Montblanc, while their lap poodles push shiny noses out of shinier Chanel handbags. They serve luscious, dark hot chocolate from Africa, that is so thick it leaves you with a foaming brown moustache like a caricature of a snooty Parisian waiter.

Let's hop back over to the left bank, crossing the Pont des Arts, groaning under the weight of all those "love locks". Drink in the view as you go, walking in the direction of St Germain in the 5th where, tucked in amongst the book and antique shops is L'Hotel. Now, Mr Rigsby would never sign MY chitty to stay here, but I urge YOU to. It's luxurious and stylish and Oscar Wilde died in Room 16. But best of all and, the height of decadence, there's a candlelit swimming pool in the basement that you can reserve for an hour all to yourself. But, hello real world, Academie St Germain (cozy, traditional) and Artus (groovy, boutiquey, ask for the mezzanine room) are both fine (and more reasonably priced) places to stay.

Wander the literary streets, browse the brimming food markets and......Do Shopping: Shakespeare and Company for books; Diptyque for candles; Grim'Art for notebooks and paper (mmmmm that dusty smell of a papetiere); Bon Marche, the grande dame of department stores and her food hall bursting with Xmas chocolate and greedy gifts.

Blimey, after all that you'll need a deep, hot bubble bath full Hermes Orange Blossom products, followed by a cocktail at the zinc bar of Alcazar. Then dinner. You might choose between......Chez Fernand in Rue Christine, all red and white tablecloths, steak with foie gras sauce, bone marrow on toast and flirting. OR, Le Comptoir – no reservations, but you can sip a Kir and nibble on succulent jambon at their wine bar next door while you wait. Yves Camdeborde, the chef, is a bit of a star but the prices are still good. You have to practically sit on one another's laps. The food is delectable and it's Paris through and through.

And I haven't even started on Le Marais, the newly restored Picasso museum, the Jardin des Plantes or mint tea at the Institut du Monde Arabe.

ALLEZ! Book a weekend. Maybe I'll see you in the dazzling mirrored bar at Le Crillon, designed by Sonia Rykiel. Mine's a dry martini (Bombay Sapphire, straight up with an olive not a twist.)

GLOSSARY

Bon Coin:
The French equivalent of Gumtree. An excellent source for second hand furniture and white goods, which can be incredibly expensive in France.

Vide Grenier:
"Empty the Loft." Held on Saturdays and Sundays in villages everywhere. Like a car boot sale but oh, so much better. Often brocanteurs and antique dealers set up stall as well. You can pick up old French treasure big and small, expensive and cheap. Do barter! It's also a good way of discovering new villages. A BBQ or a steaming vat of moules is usually on offer.

Languedoc Living:
An digital free magazine providing both local and national news. Sign up and you'll receive a daily email.

Brocante:
Antique/junk shop/second hand shop. A treasure trove of crockery, glassware, furniture, linen, books.......anything and everything.

Vendange:
Precise times vary according to the weather and the state of the grapes, but this is the

Autumnal grape harvest.

Occitanie:
The new name for the region, as voted for by the populous so they can't moan now.

Duralex:
A French brand that made the glasses used in schools. These ubiquitous little tumblers are reputedly unbreakable. V trendy these days. Not to be confused with other produits.

Vrac:
A container for a large quantity of wine – it could be a wine box or a plastic flask. You can take your own to a vintner and have it filled with your wine of choice.

Passepartout:
The loyal travelling companion in Jules Verne's "Around the World in Eighty Days." Occasionally annoying, but ultimately useful.

Concours Camarguais:
A type of bullfight particular to this area, where young men chase bulls, but do not harm them. The aim is to tie a ribbon to the horns.

Etang:
A salt water pond, a breeding ground for farmed oysters, flamingoes and copious wildlife.

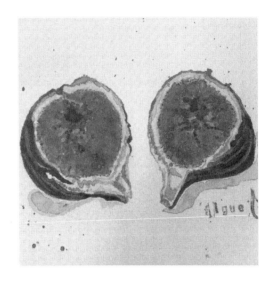

FIN

ABOUT THE AUTHOR

Judith Dowden has been a long term Francophile, ever since her first French lesson at the age of 7 years old, when Madame roared up to the school gates in a suede jacket and a red sports car. She divides her time between the Languedoc and London. As a retired Design lecturer, she is able to enrich her words with photographs and illustrations.

She looks forward to more exploration and discovery in France and that will lead to the second in the series…..

MORE MWAH